T0163217

Mordecai Schreiber

WHY

PEOPLE

PRAY

The Universal
Power of Prayer

BEAUFORT
BOOKS

Permissions:
Scripture from the Old Testament is translated
by the author from the original Hebrew.
Scripture taken from the New Testament is from the New King James
Version Copyright © 1982 by Thomas Nelson. Used by permission. All
rights reserved.
Library of Congress Cataloging-in-Publication Data On File

ISBN
paperback: 9780825308307
eBook: 9780825307577

For inquiries about volume orders, please contact:
Beaufort Books
27 West 20th Street, Suite 1102
New York, NY 10011
sales@beaufortbooks.com

Published in the United States by Beaufort Books
www.beaufortbooks.com
Distributed by Midpoint Trade Books
www.midpointtrade.com
Printed in the United States of America
Interior Design by Lorin Taylor
Cover Design by Michael Short

Mordecai Schreiber

WHY

PEOPLE

PRAY

The Universal
Power of Prayer

This book is dedicated to my
agent and my dear friend Peter Miller,
a man of faith whose friendship
and inspiration helped me bring
this book to completion.

CONTENTS

Part One: What Is Prayer
1. Why People Pray
2. What Is the Essence of Prayer?
3. Creative and Formal Prayer
4. History of Prayer
5. The Power of Words
6. Is Anyone Listening?
7. Life Is with People
8. Why Do We Need to Praise God?
9. Praying to God As a Father Figure
10. The Kaddish and the Lord's Prayer
11. Magic
12. Sacrifice
13. Prayer, Work, and Creativity
14. Meditation
15. Humility
16. Triumphalism
17. Sin
18. Suffering
19. Repentance
20. The Afterlife

Part Two: What Do People Pray for
21. Efficacy of Prayer
22. Praying for Healing
23. Praying for Prosperity
24. Lifecycle Prayers
25. Yearly Cycle Prayers
26. The Sabbath as a Day of Prayer

27. Peace of Mind
28. War
29. World Peace

Part Three - Prayer Today
30. Prayer after the Holocaust
31. The Detractors of Prayer
32. Prayer for Freethinkers
33. Prayer as a Way of Life
34. A New Language of Prayer
35. A Blueprint for the Future

PART ONE
WHAT IS PRAYER

1. WHY PEOPLE PRAY

As a rabbi, I have led people in prayer for many years and I am well aware of the emotional, spiritual, and social benefits of prayer. But I am also aware of the questioning and the outright rejection of prayer by those who doubt God or have become disillusioned with religion.

Since I retired ten years ago I had the good fortune of sailing the seven seas, first as a passenger and subsequently as a cruise rabbi. This gave me the opportunity to observe people of many different creeds and cultures engage in prayer, and I learned two important lessons about the human condition in our troubled twenty-first century: first, millions of people worldwide pray; and second, prayer is an essential human need.

I was not raised in a religious household, nor was I taught to believe that there is someone who hears prayer. I was born in the Land of Israel under the British Mandate, before it became the State of Israel. My parents and their friends had left Europe before the Great Catastrophe which, in less than four years, from June 1941 to May 1945, wiped out centuries of Jewish life, culture, and piety. They left because they no longer believed that asking God to send the long-awaited messiah would save them from the gathering storm and restore them to their Promised Land. So they stopped praying, they became secular Jews, and they went to that land on their own. They did not teach their children how to pray, because they did not believe in the power of prayer, and because they were too busy building a new state and a new society which demanded many sacrifices, and still does.

I had to discover prayer and religion on my own.

I am eternally grateful to my parents for having taken their fate into their own hands and for helping give birth to the first Jewish state in two thousand years. But from a very young age I felt connected to my ancestors who believed in God and for whom prayer was a way of life. Growing up in a land which is the cradle of world religions, I was always fascinated by prayer—not only Jewish prayer but all prayer. From early on, my understanding of prayer has been very broad, much broader than the confines of any particular "house of worship." Moreover, since I was not raised as a religious person who was taught to believe in a particular religion, it was always clear to me that prayer is universal and that the One who, to borrow the words of the Jewish prayer book, "hears prayer," hears everyone's prayer. In all of creation there is a yearning, a longing for something more than the life-giving elements of nature, such as sun, air, water, or nutrition. It is a longing to reach higher than one's limits, to become one with the source of all life. Here we may be entering the realm of mysticism, which is an expression of the human heart rather than the human mind, and which may be off-limits to science.

I consider myself a religious evolutionist. While I am a Jew who believes in God, I also believe that while God never changes, the idea of God has been evolving throughout time. Even within the Bible the idea of God evolves, from El Shaddai to Adonai to Elohim and so on. From a God who for centuries was worshiped with the offering of animal sacrifices, to a God who instead expects ethical behavior and sincere prayer. Judaism has given rise to two world religions, namely, Christianity and Islam. While all three believe in the same God, they have been at odds with one another throughout time as though they believed in different gods, which has resulted in deadly conflicts that continue to this day. I believe that a new age will dawn one day, when the entire human race will at long last realize we all believe in the same God, albeit in different ways, and that there are as many paths to God as there are human beings in this world, including non-believers, and that no one has a monopoly on God.

Whether or not one believes in God, the idea of God is the most unifying principle the world has ever known. The French philosopher Voltaire said, if God did not exist, we would have to invent God. On a recent visit to the island of Bali in Indonesia, where the prevalent religion is Hinduism, my Hindu guide explained that Hindus, though worshiping a variety of deities, believe that all of them are manifestations of the one God. The Catholic Church maintains that the trinity is three manifestations of the one God. Islam proclaims that "there is no God but God." And Judaism says, "Hear O Israel, Adonai our God, Adonai is one."

On his recent visit to the Holy Land, Pope Francis sought to initiate a reconciliation process with the Orthodox churches. I myself have been working for many years with Christian clergy on interfaith matters, and for the most part I have found my Christian colleagues to be open and anxious to reach a new age of religious coexistence. Jews and Christians share common scriptures, and have a common prayer history. There is much we can learn from each other when it comes to prayer.

I would like to take you on a journey through this primordial and essential human phenomenon known as prayer. I would like you to come along with me, without any preconceptions or bias, and see how together we can explore our personal experience of prayer. Some of us pray regularly; some of us pray occasionally; some of us dismiss prayer as a waste of time. But even those who fall into the last category find ways to pray, perhaps not in the usual sense of the word, but in ways that are not commonly associated with prayer, as we shall find out. I submit that there is no such thing as a life without prayer, whether or not one believes in a supreme being.

To live is to pray. Every day when we get up in the morning we pray for life and wellbeing for ourselves and for those we care about. We may either do so by using formal prayer, or we may simply respond to the moment of awakening when we become conscious of receiving the gift of a new day and the ability to stand up and carry on with our life. This sentiment was given one of its most beautiful expressions in a Christian hymn of Scottish origins which was made into a popular folk song by the pop singer Cat Stevens, the son of a Greek Orthodox father and Swedish Baptist mother, who himself became a Muslim in later life and who now calls himself Yusuf Islam:

Morning has broken, like the first morning,
Blackbird has spoken, like the first bird,
Praise for the singing, praise for the morning,
Praise for the springing fresh from the world.

Sweet the rain's new fall, sunlit from heaven,
Like the first dewfall, on the first grass,
Praise for the sweetness of the wet garden,
Sprung in completeness where his feet pass.

Mine is the sunlight, mine is the morning,
Born of the one light, Eden saw play.
Praise with elation, praise every morning,
God's recreation of the new day.

Here is a song that transcends any particular religion and, in effect, becomes a prayer that has a broad universal appeal. Its message is echoed in a verse in the Jewish prayer book's morning service that says that God renews every day the work of creation. The melody sung by Yusuf Islam captures perfectly that moment of awakening. It conveys the feeling of creation coming back together in an Eden-like moment, one of those moments we experience on occasions, when our mind and body and the world around us are in perfect harmony. It reminds me of a woman in my condo building in south Florida whom I see each morning walking her dog as I go for my daily swim in the ocean. After we greet each other, she usually says to me, "Another day in paradise." This too, I believe, is a prayer.

2. WHAT IS THE ESSENCE OF PRAYER?

Prayer is the expression of our deepest emotions, which are both personal and collective. Hence prayer is also personal and collective. There is a line in our emotional life which we cross when we are overcome with emotions we are not able to process, ranging from overwhelming joy to overwhelming pain. At that moment we need to reach beyond ourselves for help. I remember two such occasions in my life during my thirties. In the first instance I was on a plane flying to St. Thomas in the Caribbean to recuperate from an emotional crisis caused by my problems as a young rabbi on Long Island. I suddenly felt I was on the verge of a nervous breakdown. I did not say anything to my wife who was sitting next to me. I did not want to upset her. Instead, I gripped the armrest of my seat and suddenly I felt I was holding my mother's hand. I was a child again, and my mother was telling me to be strong, not to let myself be dragged down by my bad feelings. Slowly, I began to get a hold of myself, and I was able to calm myself down.

In the second instance I was back on Long Island sitting in my study, having just returned from Cincinnati where I had attended my father-in-law's funeral. I always felt close to my father-in-law, whom I considered my mentor and my friend, and with whom I could discuss almost anything. Suddenly I was overcome by the enormity of my loss and by his untimely departure from this world. I am not in the habit of speaking to God outside the context of prayer, but suddenly, involuntarily, I found myself saying to God in a shaking voice, "You'd better take good care of him." I had never before or since opened up my heart to God as I did at that moment.

In every religion there is a certain moment in its religious calendar when the collective emotions of its followers reach their peak. At that moment one feels the need to be together with people who share that moment, and to take part in this collective experience. For Jews, that moment is the beginning of the service on the eve of Yom Kippur, the Day of Atonement, when the cantor chants the *Kol Nidre*. At that moment Jews feel closer to God than any other time of the year. There is no rational explanation for this feeling which the Jew experiences once a year. Some might say it is rooted in fear. According to the common belief, on the eve of Yom Kippur God sits in judgment of the world and of every living soul, and man is given a twenty-four hour period, beginning at that moment, to ask for mercy, forgiveness, and the chance to make a fresh start in the New Year.

Prayer, like music and art, is the language of the heart. It is not rooted in reason, but in something beyond reason. The French philosopher Pascal said, "The heart has its reasons, which reason does not know." Sometimes, reason itself cannot reach its ultimate conclusions without having the human heart play its part in reaching those conclusions. Here I would like to quote another French philosopher, Montesquieu, who said, "With *truths* of a certain kind, it is not enough to make them appear convincing; one must also make them *felt*." It reminds me of a story I once heard told by the popular motivational speaker Wayne Dyer in one of his talks, about a woman he counseled who was always angry at her relatives. After listening to her for two years, during which time Dyer always agreed with her, he finally said to her, yes, you are always right. But are you happy? Clearly, she had let her relatives cause her to lose her serenity. She might have been perfectly logical, but she could have been more tolerant and forgiving and would have spared herself a great deal of unnecessary grief. I once had a relative who went through life behaving like that woman. My relative was almost always angry at someone. She rarely smiled. She paid a high price for always being right.

One of the objectives of prayer is to remind us that we cannot always be right. We live in an imperfect world. We all have our shortcomings and limitations, and therefore we have to know how to forgive others and give them some wiggle room. In other words, prayer, which taps into our innermost soul, teaches us humility. The very act of praying is the acceptance of the fact that we are not all-powerful. We need help to be able to cope with those things in life which may overwhelm us. We need to be able to let go and step outside of ourselves to enter the place where we feel the presence of something greater than ourselves that can give us the "serenity to accept the things we cannot change," and "the courage to change the things we can." Putting our lives in perspective is what prayer does. Once our body and soul are in harmony with the world around us, we can embrace life and live what is known as the "good life."

Prayer is many things and it manifests itself in many ways. One way of understanding the wide range of prayer is by considering the element of sound as it relates to prayer. One example of this range of sound is found in the biblical story of the prophet Elijah escaping to the desert where he hears the voice of God:

So God said, "Go forth and stand on the mountain before God." And behold, God was passing by. And a great and strong wind was rending the mountains and breaking in pieces the rocks before God, but God was not in the wind. And after the wind an earthquake, but God was not in the earthquake. After the earthquake a fire, but the God was not in the fire; and after the fire a sound of a still small voice. *When Elijah heard it, he wrapped his face in his mantle and went out and stood at the entrance of the cave. And behold, a voice came to him and said, "What are you doing here, Elijah?" (I Kings 19:11-13)*

God appears to Elijah in the deafening sound of a rock-breaking strong wind, an earthquake, and a fire. But when Elijah finally hears the voice of God it is in a "still small voice." The same is true of the prayer experience in many cultures, past and present. Christian prayer runs the sound gamut from loud church bells to silent meditation. Muslims are called to prayer by the muezzin, but when they pray during the daytime it is typically silent. Jewish prayer ranges from chanting in unison, with the voice of the cantor usually reaching high decibels, to the silent reading of the Amidah, or the silent prayer, which is the most important prayer of the Jewish ritual.

The range of sound in American prayer is perhaps broader than most. Having attended prayer services in many different American houses of worship, I was particularly struck by two very different sound levels. The loudest I can recall has been in African American evangelical churches, where the choir and the pastor rock the church with their loud singing, clapping and dancing. The most quiet prayer experience I recall was a Quaker religious service or meeting where people sat in silent meditation for a long time, with one person occasionally getting up and saying something, apparently "moved by the spirit." I have found both to be deeply spiritual. Like Elijah's encounter with God in the desert, it begins with a storm, but it ends with "a still small voice."

3. CREATIVE AND FORMAL PRAYER

Before there were prayer books, there was creative or spontaneous prayer. When we go back to the biblical text and to the ancient texts of civilizations that precede the Bible by many centuries, we find prayers spoken or written by individuals, some renowned and some ordinary, who address God or the gods, and whose words have been preserved throughout the ages for us to read and ponder. One example of a spontaneous prayer in the Bible is that of a woman who pours her heart out before God. Her name is Hannah, the mother of the prophet Samuel. Hannah is one of the two wives of a man called Elkanah, who lives in the Land of Canaan in the time of the Judges. The other wife, Pnina, is blessed with children, while Hannah is barren. When Elkanah takes his wives and children to the house of God in Shiloh, Hannah is overcome with grief for being barren and addresses God as follows,

> *O God of hosts, if you will indeed look on the affliction of your handmaiden and remember me, and not forget your handmaiden, but will give your handmaiden a male child, then I will give him to God all the days of his life, and there shall no razor come upon his head. (I Samuel 11)*

After God blesses Hannah with a child who will become the great prophet Samuel, Hannah thanks God with a long prayer reminiscent of the Psalms, which looks like a later insertion in the body of the story, and is not quite the prayer of an ordinary woman. But it is the above-cited prenatal prayer which comes directly from the heart of an afflicted woman who speaks to God and makes a vow. If Hannah lived in post-biblical times, she might very well have recited from the Book of Psalms, which Jews and others have turned to for the past twenty centuries in seeking help from God. But in her day one spoke directly to God and made personal petitions.

It appears that Judaism over the centuries has formalized prayer down to the smallest details of everyday life. There is a prayer for nearly every moment of the day, for every kind of food, and for every human activity. To this day, the life of a strictly observant Jew revolves constantly around formal prayer. There is little room left for spontaneous, heartfelt prayer. Everything seems to be preordained, as if the sages of the past have done all the thinking for the rest of us, and all a pious Jews has to do is keep repeating the words they bequeathed us long ago.

There is only one little problem. In recent decades the world has changed more than it has in centuries. While formal Jewish prayer has evolved over the years, it has not evolved enough to satisfy the needs of today's world. While this is true about traditional Jewish prayer, it is also true in regard to much of its Muslim equivalent. Here the entire dynamic of the ritual, including washing before prayer, bodily gestures, and the text and recitation of the prayers themselves are rigidly applied. The individual seems to dissolve during the five daily prayer periods into the mass of worshipers around him and be deprived of personal freedom to address his maker about his own specific concerns.

In Islam this has not always been the case. In the late

fourteenth century the city of Damascus in today's Syria came under siege. The situation was very precarious, and the local Muslim scholar Muhammad al-Jazri composed a prayer for peace, which could be used in today's Syria which is being ravaged by a particularly savage conflict:

O Allah, unite our hearts
and set aright our mutual affairs.
Guide us in the path of peace.
Liberate us from darkness by Your light.
Save us from enormities whether open or hidden.
Bless us in our ears, eyes, hearts, spouses, and
children.
Turn to us; truly you are Oft-Returning, Most Merciful.
Make us grateful for Your bounty and full of praise for
it
so that we may continue to receive it
and complete Your blessings upon us.

Of the three so-called Abrahamic religions, Christianity appears to have put the most emphasis on spontaneous or creative prayer. Neither Catholic nor Protestant liturgy is as static as the other two. The Catholic ritual may be more formal than the Protestant. But it is common in Christian liturgy in general to let the individual believer recite prayers spontaneously, as in the case of saying grace before a meal. Here are a few examples of Christian grace before meals:

Catholic:

a.
Bless us,
O Lord,
and these your gifts,
which we are about to receive
from your bounty
Through Christ our Lord.
Amen.

b.
Lord Jesus, our brother,
We praise You for saving us.
Bless us in Your love As we gather in your Name,
And bless this meal that we share.
Jesus, we praise you forever.
Amen.

c.
Father of us all,
this meal is a sign of Your love for us.
Bless us and bless our food,
And help us to give you glory each day
Through Jesus Christ our Lord.
Amen!

Protestant:

a.
For food in a world where many walk in hunger,

For faith in a world where many walk in fear;
For friends in a world where many walk alone
We give you thanks, O Lord.

b.
Bless the Lord, O my soul,
And all that is within me, bless his holy name.
Bless the Lord, O my soul,
And forget not all his benefits.
Blessed be God, eternal king,
for these and all his good gifts to us.

c.
O Lord, we thank you for the gifts of
your bounty which we enjoy at this table.
As you have provided for us in the past,
so may you sustain us throughout our lives.
While we enjoy your gifts,
may we never forget the needy
and those in want.

Among Jews, the Jewish Reform movement and to a lesser extent the Conservative movement, have done a great deal of work in recent years in the area of creative prayer. The Reform prayer book has undergone several revisions in the past fifty years. The most recent version offers several alternative services for the Sabbath. The Passover Haggadah has been modernized. The four matriarchs of the Jewish people (Sarah, Rebecca, Leah and Rachel) have been added to the Amidah prayer, along with the three patriarchs (Abraham, Isaac and Jacob). Moses' sister, Miriam, is now mentioned in the prayers. New readings by contemporary writers have been included. And thanks to innovative liturgical composers like Debbie Friedman, new melodies have been added for the key prayers, which have greatly enhanced the service.

All the major religions have a rich literature of creative and innovative prayers. More of those need to be added to the service in keeping with the zeitgeist, or the spirit of the time. Another innovative feature of contemporary prayer is the use of musical instruments other than the traditional organ. Here again this signifies a return to biblical times, when the ritual at the Holy Temple in Jerusalem included several musical instruments such as trumpets, lyres, tambourines, cymbals and more. Given the prominence of popular music in today's world, especially among the young, this addition is vital for bringing the youth into the house of prayer.

Not all innovative prayer represents an improvement over formal prayer. This is the reason why movements like Reform Judaism have felt compelled in recent years to keep putting out new versions of their prayer books. But all of this is for the good. Formal prayer always runs the risk of stagnation. Life is not static, and religion has to keep up with the times.

4. HISTORY OF PRAYER

Every major religion has its holy books which over time become the inspiration and the source of formal prayer for that particular religion. While I derive inspiration and life wisdom from many of those books, my own source of prayer is the Hebrew *Tanach*, which Christians call the Old Testament and which I prefer to call the Hebrew Scriptures or simply the Bible. I do not consider the Bible to be merely a human document, written by human authors over time. One of the best-known texts of the Hebrew Bible is the 23rd Psalm, which is part of the Book of Psalms, one of the books included in the third part of the Hebrew Bible, known as the Wisdom Literature. No other book in history has provided more prayers and more spiritual inspiration than the Book of Psalms. Every Jewish and every Christian service includes one or more Psalms. Expressions such as "Hallelujah" or "Praise the Lord" or "Amen," which are familiar to both Jews and Christians, are derived from the Book of Psalms. One could make a good case for calling this book the main source of humankind's language of prayer.

To me, the Bible is a divinely inspired book. The biblical prophets, from Moses to Malachi, are to me the ones who heard and transmitted to us the word of God. Their teachings are reflected in the teachings of all the other major religions around the world, and affirm the universality of faith. I have been taught and have studied the Bible on my own since the first grade, and I have never grown tired of it. We sing in our Sabbath morning service, "It is a tree of life to them who hold fast to it, and those who support it are happy." Indeed, a tree of life. One never grows tired of eating the fruit of a nourishing tree. By the same token, I have never grown tired of reading and studying the Torah and using its words in prayer. The older I get, the more meaning I find in its pages. I agree with the Psalmist who says, "Where it not for Your Torah, my delight, I would have long been lost in my affliction."

The book of prayer of any faith is a derivative of that faith's scriptures, which are attributed to a higher source. Its purpose is to enable the praying person to communicate with that higher source and transition, so to speak, from the material world with all of its toil and trouble to a higher spiritual world where one may find harmony, peace, and mental fortitude, and be able to live a life "in God's image." Man is a thinking animal, and man uses words to articulate thoughts. The words of the prayer book are organized around the unifying principle of faith, which recognizes a cosmic force that enables man to fulfill the potential of becoming a person who is created in the divine image.

But there are many other sources of prayer besides the original scriptures of the great religions. Within the great religions of the east and the west, a variety of religious movements have emerged over the centuries down to our own time, such as the Zen movement of Buddhism in China, the Sufi movement of Islam in Persia, the Hasidic movement of Judaism in Eastern Europe, and the Mormon movement of Christianity in the United States. All those movements have enriched the prayer life of the mother religion with their own prayers (meditation in the case of Zen), and have reinvigorated the spiritual life of millions.

In addition, religious hymns and songs composed

throughout the centuries have become an essential part of the prayer book. The most solemn chant of the Jewish liturgy is *Kol Nidre*, intoned on the eve of the Day of Atonement. It is not a formal prayer, because it does not address God. It is actually a meditation and an expression of contrition and regret for human failings. Its exact origins are not known, but it was composed several centuries after biblical times, not in Hebrew but in Aramaic, a language Jews spoke during Talmudic and post-Talmudic time in the Middle East.

Another post-biblical traditional song is *Lecha dodi*, sung every week on the eve of the Sabbath. It was composed in the sixteenth century in the town of Safed in the Galilee by Shlomo Alkabetz, a Kabbalist, or Jewish mystic. Nothing conveys the spiritual essence of the Sabbath and its centrality in Jewish faith better than this hymn.

An example of a two-century-old English hymn that has become one of the best known and loved Christian hymns, mostly in the United States where it has also become a popular African American spiritual, is Amazing Grace. It is a moving hymn of redemption written by John Newton, an English sea captain who was engaged in the African slave trade, and later became an Anglican minister and a poet who advocated the abolition of slavery in England, which came to fruition in 1807 right before he died, almost sixty years ahead of the United States:

> *Amazing Grace, how sweet the sound*
> *That saved a wretch like me.*
> *I once was lost but now am found*
> *Was blind, but now I see.*

Here again, as in the case of *Kol Nidre*, it is the melody that seems to have contributed to the great emotional impact which has captivated people of many different backgrounds for the past two hundred years. Clearly, music and song have always been an integral part of communal prayer, as attested by the following Psalm:

> *Praise God with the sounding of the trumpet,*
> *Praise God with the harp and lyre,*
> *Praise God with tambourine and dancing,*
> *Praise God with the strings and flute,*
> *Praise God with the clash of cymbals,*
> *Praise God with resounding cymbals.*
> *Let everything that has breath praise God.*
> *Hallelujah. (Psalms 150:3-6)*

What we have seen so far is that prayer is a universal cultural phenomenon that originates at a particular point in time with a particular person who experiences what one may call a moment of transformation, born of what Buddhists may call illumination, or Christians an epiphany, or Jews a *gilui shechinah*, or divine revelation. At such a moment a person may utter or write down a prayer which may captivate the heart of the listener or the reader, and if that particular prayer continues to inspire people, it will eventually find its way into the prayer language of one or more religious movements.

5. THE POWER OF WORDS

Prayer is based on the premise that words have the power to affect the outcome of events, and that certain words, especially the ones we find in a prayer book, when intoned by the praying person with an open heart can be heard and have an effect. In the Book of Genesis, we are told that God created the world using the power of the spoken word ("And God said, let there be light, and there was light.") In the New Testament we read:

> In the beginning was the Word.
> And the Word was with God, and the Word was God.
> . .
> And the Word was made flesh, and dwelled among us.
> (John 1:1, 14)

While words are what makes us human, they are believed to make us more than human. Words can heal, and words can kill. Words can create, and words can destroy. Words can bring out the worst in us, but they can also bring out the best in us. Certain texts, dating back centuries and even millennia, have never been surpassed. Human morality is still based on the Ten Commandments. Philosophy is still based on the teachings of Plato and Aristotle. Poetry goes back to Homer's Iliad and Odyssey. The novel begins with Cervantes' *Don Quijote*, still perhaps the greatest novel ever written. The plays of Shakespeare have never been surpassed. And no book ever written has given the world more spiritual comfort and inspiration than the Hebrew Book of Psalms.

Many things change over time. Science and technology, for example, have progressed since the times of Moses, Jesus, Plato, Shakespeare, and Cervantes beyond anything those giants of the human spirit could have ever imagined. But the same Bible some of them read and lived by is still with us today. This, when we think about it, is truly remarkable. Why would words written thousands of years ago when the world was scientifically and technologically so far behind today's world still inspire us? What kind of power do those words possess, and where does it come from?

One can be a believer or a non-believer. But no one can deny the power that words spoken and written by the founders of the great religions and by their successors still hold sway over millions of people everywhere on this planet. Who in the West a hundred years ago would have imagined that the words spoken by the Buddha in India and by other great teachers in the East over two thousand years ago would make such inroads among Westerners in the late twentieth century? People in the West, seeking peace of mind and harmony with the world around them, do not turn to scientific writings of any kind, but to the teachings of Eastern religions, such as the varieties of meditation practiced by Zen and Tao and other meditative disciplines, as an alternative to traditional Western prayer. More on this in the chapter on prayer and meditation.

The power of words does not reside in the words themselves. Words listed in a dictionary do not inspire. What infuses words with power is the ideas they express or the emotions they evoke. The power of the words in the texts of the various faiths stems from the fact that they express timeless verities about the great questions of life, and give people solace and fortitude as they face life's struggles and the ultimate reality of death. They represent not only the original ideas of the founders of the faith, but also the cumulative wisdom their successors recorded in the course of time. Whether it is the Sufis in Islam, or Maimonides in Judaism, or St. Thomas Aquinas or St. Teresa of Avila in Christianity, we are the heirs to all that rich tradition that reflects the wisdom and insights of those luminaries. The words they have bequeathed us continue to inspire us and enrich our lives.

Judaism and Christianity are both founded on the words of the Hebrew Bible, which Christians call the Old Testament. In some schools today the Bible is taught as literature rather than as a sacred text. Indeed, the Hebrew Bible contains great literature, including great poetry, storytelling, aphorisms, and drama. But this only puts it on par with classic literature of Greek and Rome and the rest of Europe. But while the classics continue to thrill us and enrich our lives, they do not teach us how to live the good life or how to find comfort and fortitude as we encounter life's hardships. Not all words were created equal. Some words only tell us how to get from here to there or how to operate a device. Some words make us laugh or cry. But the scriptures of the great religions teach us how to live a life of tranquility and righteousness.

Many have wondered how a small people like the Jews who have been dispersed all over the world and for some twenty centuries did not have their own land were able to survive to this day. The answer is very simple. The Jews have a book that narrates their early history, tells them how for centuries they have overcome all odds, gives them rules to live by, and helps them find fortitude in times of trouble. This book, which is the most influential book ever written is the secret of Jewish survival. It is called the Bible.

One may wonder what human life on this planet would have been like without the scriptures of the great religions and without prayer. All one has to do is study the history of pagan antiquity. I cannot think of too many people who would like to go back to those days. With all its faults and shortcomings, religion has and still does provide the words people live by, and will continue to live by for a long time to come.

6. IS ANYONE LISTENING?

But what happens when we pray? Are we talking to ourselves, or is someone listening? Normally when we speak we address our words to someone who listens and responds. When we pray, it appears we are speaking to ourselves. When we pray in a group, we hear others pray, and in a way we are addressing one another. Some formal prayers are written as a dialogue. The leader says something, and the group responds. This is called a responsive prayer. But the great mystery is whether there is something greater than ourselves that hears the prayer and has the power to take action and grant us whatever it is we are asking for.

A very good case can be made that prayer is actually a form of a pep talk we give ourselves, which someone has referred to as the "power of positive thinking." Our daily lives are full of negative feelings such as dismay, frustration and anger, which are the result of what seems to be the constant struggle life imposes on us. These negative feelings linger on and weigh us down, depriving us of our peace of mind, and making us worry and feel unhappy and inadequate. A good example of a contemporary prayer that is designed to restore our peace of mind is the "Serenity Prayer," which, for one thing, was adopted by the organization Alcoholics Anonymous. It goes somewhat like this:

> *God, grant me the serenity to accept the things I*
> *cannot change,*
> *the courage to change the things I can,*
> *and the wisdom to know the difference.*

Years ago, when I first came across this prayer, it made perfect sense to me. It is one example of the many prayers, poems, meditations, and inspired words I have found over the years in many cultures and religions, ancient and contemporary, which have enriched what I would call my "prayer life." Notice that the above-cited "Serenity Prayer" is addressed to God. But in reality it makes just as much sense if you simply address it to yourself. Serenity, courage and wisdom are qualities that would enrich anyone's life, believer and nonbeliever alike. The same is true of the song "Morning Has Broken." While it alludes to the biblical story of creation and attributes creation to God in its last verse, it is actually a song about nature renewing itself with every new day, and here too it does not seem to matter whether one is marveling at nature as a divine creation or simply as the most marvelous thing known to man. One can wonder whether God exists. But it is hard to find someone who wonders whether nature exists.

But the question still remains: Is anyone listening?

To me, the two above-cited examples of what appears to be universal prayer make it clear that prayer is a good thing whether or not someone is actually listening. The song about the new morning offers a wonderful opportunity to appreciate and celebrate life renewing itself as we start a new day, especially when we are fortunate enough to be in good health, and we can hear the song of birds and breathe fresh air in a beautiful garden after a rainfall, as the morning sun begins to warm up the earth. It is at that moment that one feels like saying "thank you," thanking one's good fortune and, if one feels the need to go a step further, thanking also the source of life, that mysterious force that keeps breathing new life into nature with every new day.

The same is true of the prayer asking for serenity, courage, and wisdom. Whether one says these words as a pep-talk to oneself, or whether one begins with the word "God," it is the outcome that matters. The very act of asking for those things is an act of positive thinking, and if indeed there is a higher force that can enhance those qualities in us, so much the better. If one is to ask, does it really help? The answer is: it certainly doesn't hurt.

The answer to the question "is anyone listening," is this: it is a matter of faith. It is left to each one of us to answer it to ourselves. Sometimes we feel someone is listening, and sometimes we don't. But over time we form a basic belief or disbelief. We either believe or we don't believe that someone may be listening. We can also find ourselves in the middle, not knowing what to believe. But again, no matter which of those three basic categories we belong to, the above two examples show that prayer is useful not only for some, but for everyone.

My own answer, which came to me over time, is yes. Yes, someone is indeed listening. The world is not a free for all. It is not an accident. There is a reason and a purpose for everything. This idea of a reason and a purpose is found in the popular American folk song of the fifties and sixties, which derives its words from the biblical book of Ecclesiastes:

> *There is a time and a season for everything under the heavens:*
> *a time to be born and a time to die, a time to plant and a time to uproot,*

a time to kill and a time to heal, a time to tear down
and a time to build. (Ecclesiastes 3:1-3)

The sun rises and the sun sets, and hurries back to
where it rises. The wind blows to the southand turns to
the north; round and round it goes, ever returning on its
course. (Ibid. 1:5-6)

The earth turns around itself, and it also turns around the sun. Something here was set in motion, and this motion gives us day and night, it gives us the seasons, and it gives us life. Yes, we do know that our planet is but a grain of sand in the vast universe. But, as we were told by the great English poet and mystic, William Blake:

To see a World in a Grain of Sand
And a Heaven in a Wild Flower,
Hold infinity in the palm of your hand
And Eternity in an hour.

We have never seen infinity, and we cannot measure eternity. But these are concepts which the human mind has been able to extrapolate from the finite and temporal world we know. By the same token, it is not given to mere mortals to see God, and yet here too we have created the concept of God from the limitations of our own human knowledge.

To believe that someone hears human prayer is to believe in a creator who continues to be aware of the human condition. My long experience of living with and working with people who either believe or do not believe has taught me that faith is not something every human being is born with. Some are, some are not. For as long as I can remember, I have always felt a presence in my life which transcended the here and now. Over time, as my life experience and my knowledge kept growing, this presence became more and more pronounced. It grew deeper and stronger, and it has become an integral part of my inner life. It became clear to me that the God experience is very personal and very different with each one of us who believe. This is something which the Sages of the Talmud understood when they said that the Bible does not refer to the God of Abraham, Isaac and Jacob, but rather talks about "the God of Abraham, the God of Isaac, and the God of Jacob." Not because they are three different deities, but because each person has a different understanding and a different relationship with the one God.

I have a confession to make. Religion teaches us to fear God. A God-fearing person is someone who believes in God. But while I believe in God, it has never occurred to me to be afraid to do or not to do something because God is watching and if I do the wrong thing or fail to do the right thing God will punish me. It is clear to me that God expects me to do the right thing, and I try to do what I believe to be the right thing. I believe that the concept of "fearing God" is easily misunderstood. The idea of fear implies that something or someone is about to harm us, and we have to be vigilant and take measures to put ourselves out of danger. This cannot possibly be what is meant by the "fear of God." It does not mean fearing someone who is waiting to punish us. The Bible makes this clear when it says that God does not wait to punish the wayward person. Instead, God is waiting for that person to turn back to the right path and shun evil.

Thus, "fearing God" does not mean physical fear but rather reverence, respect, and acceptance of God's will.

My religion teaches me to love God "with all my heart and with all my soul and with all my might." As best I can tell, I do love God. But more importantly, my deepest feeling towards God is one of friendship. I think of God as a friend or, better yet, a friendly teacher. God to me is both the ultimate teacher and the ultimate friend. Normally, we do not fear a friend, quite the contrary. A friend is someone we trust and feel safe with. The thought of God as my friend is very comforting to me, and it sustains me, especially in my hour of need. It reminds me of the words of the author of the Book of Psalms, which have comforted so many people and still do:

God is my shepherd, I know no want.
He makes me to lie down in green pastures:
He leads me beside the still waters,
He restores my soul.
He leads me in paths of righteousness for His name's
sake.
Yeah, though I walk through the valley of the shadow
of death,
I will fear no evil, for You are with me;
Your rod and your staff they comfort me.
You prepare a table before me in the presence of my
enemies;
You anoint my head with oil; my cup runs over.
Surely goodness and mercy shall follow me all the days
of my life,
And I shall dwell in God's house for many years.

This Psalm is recited by both Jews and Christians during a time of bereavement, and it refers to God as what we might call the "good shepherd," who is also a good friend. There is a beautiful line in Christian hymns which describes the Christian Savior as the one who "walks with me and talks with me," as indeed a good friend does. This is exactly how I feel when I think of the one who spoke and the world came into being. I find myself calling on God as you would call on a friend when I am either overwhelmed with pain or with happiness. In the first instance, I ask for help. In the second, I express my gratitude.

I am not in any way trying to convince anyone that what I believe or do is right and what someone else believes or does is wrong. There is no right or wrong when it comes to what one feels or thinks about God. There is only the single human being all alone facing the ultimate mystery of God. Every religion understands that the ultimate reality of God is beyond human understanding. The prophet known as the Second Isaiah tells us regarding God: "For my thoughts are not your thoughts, and your ways are not my ways." (55:8) There is an unbridgeable divide between the human and the divine.

If you want to trivialize my idea of God as a personal friend, you could call it an infantile notion, similar to what very young children conceive of as an imaginary friend. There may very well be a connection between the two. I do believe that there is a child living inside every adult person, the child that person once was, who continues to inform one's life. I personally do not recall having an imaginary friend when I was a young child. What I do recall is that I was raised by a loving father whom I always considered my friend, and perhaps this is where my idea of God as a friend was formed. The great French writer Honoré de Balzac in his novel Father Goriot has his character, the old Goriot, who reminds me of King Lear, say regarding his ungrateful daughters: "When I became a father I understood God." The God I have come to know and understand is one who craves human friendship, and when one shows what God would consider to be ingratitude, God suffers, as we would suffer if a friend disappointed us.

I do believe that there is a seeing eye and a listening ear. How God responds to prayer is beyond our understanding. But prayer, as a basic human need, is not hard to understand. It seems to be deeply embedded in the human soul, and it is expressed in different ways by different people.

7. LIFE IS WITH PEOPLE

There is a vast difference between personal prayer and communal prayer. As we shall see in the ensuing chapters, there are many ways one can tap into one's soul and reach a state of prayer. For example, the person who plants a tree or paints a landscape is giving expression to his or her own personal relation with the transcendent. But all of our personal life experience grows out of our communal experience. It begins with our parents and those we are related to, and it continues with our community, friends, teachers and all the people we meet on the path of life, all of whom shape our identity, our beliefs and our behavior.

Most people are shaped by their ancestral origins, which help form their beliefs and their spiritual life. Nowhere have I found this to be truer than in my travels in Southeast Asia, particularly in Vietnam, which is a country that practices several Eastern religions, including Buddhism. When I first traveled to Vietnam a few years ago, I happened to arrive there during the Chinese New Year, which is observed by the Vietnamese people as an important traditional holiday. As I traveled from Saigon, or Ho Chi Minh City, to Hanoi, I saw thousands of people traveling mainly on motorbikes to visit their ancestors' graves. Ancestor worship is one of the main aspects of Chinese and Southeastern Asian cultures. Its history reaches back to both the ancient Greeks and the ancient Hebrews. One of the key beliefs in Judaism is that The Jews are protected by God because of the merit of their ancestors, Abraham, Isaac and Jacob. When the Jew prays, he reminds God of the merit of the fathers as a way to get God's attention.

In biblical times, the most important worship events were the three pilgrimages to Jerusalem the Hebrews undertook during the pilgrimage festivals, Sukkot (Tabernacles), Pesach (Passover), and Shavuot (Pentecost). Vast crowds gathered at the Temple Mount to make offerings to God, to celebrate historical events such as the exodus from Egypt, and to give thanks for the harvest. Similar gatherings take place to this day in the Muslim world, when thousands gather in Mecca from the entire Muslim world, and in the Christian world, when thousands of Catholics from around the world gather at the Vatican to receive a blessing from the pope.

Participation in communal prayer is an affirmation of common beliefs, common sacred texts, common rituals, and a common channel linking the human to the divine, which are shared by those who come together to pray as a community. In communal prayer, one becomes more than just oneself. Formal prayer includes prayers in both the first person singular and in the first person plural, as one prays both as "I" and as "we." The reason for this is that while participating in communal prayer, one does not cease to be a distinctive person who continues to have a distinctive relationship with the transcendent. But the transformative power of prayer is its ability to change the solitary "I" into the communal "we." This can only happen when people come together to pray as a community. The cumulative power of communal prayer is greater than the power of personal prayer. Even when one prays as "I," one is still praying in the context of "we." Ultimately, no one is simply "I." Everyone is part of "we," whether or not that person actually takes part in formal prayer.

In Israel today, less than 30 percent of Israeli Jews attend prayer services, while the remaining 70 percent do not. But even among the nonobservant a majority sees prayer and tradition as part of its patrimony, and identifies with the prayer life of the country.

The history of Hebrew and Jewish prayer focuses on the community. When the Ten Commandments were brought down from Mount Sinai by Moses and the voice of God was heard, it was heard by the entire People of Israel who were present at the foot of the mountain. A direct bond was established between God and the people, and to find one's way back to God, one has to turn to the community. Over time, the smallest community unit for the purposes of Jewish prayer will be defined as ten people, or a *minyan*. To have a full prayer experience, a quorum of at least ten has to be formed. The traditional Jewish belief is that a solitary prayer may or may not be heard, but a prayer by ten or more supplicants is always heard. Community in Judaism is everything, as it is in all major religions. "Do not separate yourself from the community," the Talmud reminds the Jew. If it is a choice between praying alone or forming part of a quorum, the Jew is expected to join the quorum.

The same concept can be applied to both learning and good deeds. One can learn alone, but nothing can replace a good teacher, or, for that matter, studying with a friend or with a group. As we shall see, study is a form of prayer, and communal study is comparable to communal prayer. When the Torah is read in the synagogue, it is in effect a Torah lesson shared by the entire assemblage.

Vox populi vox Dei: the voice of the people is the voice of God. This is an old saying of unclear origin. But it embodies a great truth which is yet to be fully explored. One of the great secrets of prayer is the secret of how to listen to the voice of other people and recognize the voice of God. An example of the "voice of the people is the voice of God" can be found in a Hasidic short story told by the Yiddish writer Sholem Asch, about a Jewish shepherd boy named Yashek who never learned how to read and write or how to pray, but to whom God was ever-present in his life. On Yom Kippur this boy went into the synagogue and heard the people pouring their heart before God. Unable to join their prayer but feeling their fear and anxiety, the boy put two fingers in his mouth and let out a loud whistle. Startled, the people looked at him in anger and asked the rabbi to expel him from the holy assembly. The rabbi looked up and said, where is that holy person who, with his whistle, opened the gates of heaven for our prayers to come before the throne of God? They looked for him, but he had slipped away and went back to his flock.

Life is with people. Ultimately, praying alone and only for one's own interest misses the deeper significance of prayer. Prayer is not about self-interest. It is about selflessness. By helping others we help ourselves. By ignoring the needs of others, we hurt ourselves.

Hillel the Elder said, "If I am not for myself, who is for me? But if I am only for myself, what am I?" There are those who rely solely on themselves and do not see the need to rely on others. And there are those who only rely on others, but not on themselves. Either extreme is contrary to the spirit of prayer. While prayer is not about self-interest, it is about striking a balance in one's life between overreliance on one's self and overreliance on others. Religion, when practiced without abdicating one's right to question, is not about blind obedience. It is about having faith and reason at the same time. In the stories of creation in Genesis it is made clear that man was given a body and a mind to be used in taking charge of life on this earth. It means, above all, the freedom to make decisions, and the imperative of making the right decisions.

8. Why Do We Need to Praise God?

It appears that throughout time mortals have found it necessary to praise God in order to get God's attention and have their prayers answered. For the skeptics among us, this raises the question whether God actually needs all that praise and adulation to be responsive to human needs. I am not a skeptic, but it is clear to me that an all-powerful God does not need the praise of mere mortals. Here again I go back to the idea of the "power of positive thinking." The purpose of praising God is not to make God feel good. It is to put ourselves in a positive state of mind as we face life's daily challenges and the tasks we undertake to do. My father once told me that back in Eastern Europe where he grew up in a traditional Jewish home, he was taught never to curse. If you feel an urge to curse, he was told, say a blessing instead. Instead of saying "damn you," say "bless you." As I recall, while he was not a praying Jew, he always used to say "bless" instead of "damn."

The Talmud teaches us that prayer in and of itself is of little value. It only takes on meaning if it leads to good deeds. Prayer is not an end but a means. God does not need to be praised or, going back in time, to be regaled with ritual offerings such as animal sacrifices and incense. Like parents who love their children, God's greatest wish is to have those children treat one another with kindness and compassion. One of my favorite expressions of this truth is found in the New Testament where it says, "Whatever you do to the least of my brothers, you do to Me."

Prayer as an act of praising God is not an end in itself. To praise God is to reaffirm our resolve to do what God expects of us. To say "Thank you, God," is to make a commitment to "repair and perfect the world in God's image." This is a task which has faced man since the beginning of time, and still does.

How often does one need to praise God? This raises the question of repetitive prayer as opposed to praying when one feels the need to pray. Religion prescribes a set prayer schedule. Whether it is a Muslim who prays five times a day, or a Jew who prays three times a day, or a Christian who essentially attends church on Sunday and prays on a more personal level during the week (Christianity actually believes in seven daily prayer periods), repetitive or scheduled prayer is a common practice. The question is, how effective is repetitive prayer?

The problem with repetitive prayer is that it often becomes rote, a routine activity. In that case, prayer may become mechanical, unfeeling, and of questionable value. One may wonder: is it desirable to offer praise to God repetitively, even though it is often a mechanical act, or to do so only when one is moved to offer such praise?

The answer can be found in a verse from the book of Psalms: "I have set God before me *always*." (16:8) Clearly, one cannot always pray effectively. But what one can do, if one can find a way to let God into one's life, is *be in an ongoing relationship with* God. We all have our human relationships with people we know and whose lives we share. We don't praise them every moment, but they are in our thoughts and we are concerned about their welfare. Here again we can quote the Psalms: "For the sake of my brothers and friends, I will say, 'Peace be within you.'" (122:8) We do not praise God only with words of prayer, but also with our inner thoughts and feelings, and with our state of mind. If God is a constant partner in our lives, our act of praising God is ongoing and sincere at all times whether or not we engage in repetitive prayer.

Seen from this broad perspective, we can see how prayer, as an act of praising God, reaches far beyond any formal or repetitive ritual. First and foremost, acts of kindness are a form of prayer. Treating other people as God's children is the greatest gift one can give God. Mistreating people, and showing disregard for human life, is the worse offense against God one may commit.

One of the most beautiful stories I have ever come across in Jewish lore which drives home the point that prayer is of little consequence without acts of kindness, is the Hasidic story about the righteous Rabbi of Nemerov. This story is best known in the version told by I. L. Peretz, called "If Not Higher." Here is a summary of the story.

Every year before the High Holy Days, the rabbi of Nemerov would disappear. Instead of joining his followers in the penitential prayers in preparation for the Days of Awe, he would be gone and could not be found. Where did he go? The rabbi, His devoted followers explained, went to heaven to ask God for forgiveness for their sins.

This answer did not sit well with a certain Litvak, a religious skeptic who found the Hasidim to be naïve. He decided to find out for himself, and so he travelled to Nemerov to spy on the rabbi. The Litvak arrived in Nemerov during the night and lay in wait for the rabbi. Before dawn he saw the rabbi emerge from his house dressed like a Russian peasant. In the pre-dawn light, he followed him into the woods on the edge of the town. The rabbi took out an ax and chopped some firewood. He tied the wood and carried the stack on his shoulder as he marched toward town.

The Litvak kept following the rabbi at a short distance and saw him reach the door of a small shack. The rabbi knocked on the door and an old woman's voice was heard asking who was there.

The rabbi answered in Russian, letting her know his name was Vasil. She asked him what he wanted, and he replied he had some cheap wood to sell. The old woman sighed and said she was old and sick and could not afford the wood. The rabbi assured her he was in no hurry to be paid, and if he could trust her, she could certainly trust the Almighty who helps the needy. But I am all alone and I am too frail to light the fire, she insisted. Not to worry, the rabbi said, I will light it for you.

As the rabbi was lighting the fire, he softly sang the penitential prayers while the Litvak was watching through the window.

When the Litvak went back to his town and his friends asked him whether the rabbi actually went to heaven, the Litvak, who became a follower of the rabbi, replied, he most certainly went up to heaven, if not higher.

The poor woman alone in her shack needed help. By providing that help at a time when his followers expected their rabbi to lead them in prayer at the most solemn time of the year, the rabbi was praising God by doing God's work. Certainly good works are a form of prayer.

In Buddhism, we find a shift of emphasis from prayer to

good deeds. A widely quoted Buddhist prayer is the Metta Koruna Prayer, which is one of the most beautiful prayers I have ever come across:

O Amida Buddha,
Oneness of Life and Light,
Entrusting in your Great Compassion,
May you shed the foolishness in myself,
Transforming me into a conduit of Love.
May I be a medicine for the sick and weary,
Nursing their afflictions until they are cured;
May I become food and drink,
During time of famine,
May I protect the helpless and the poor,
May I be a lamp for those who need your Light,
May I be a bed for those who need rest,
and guide all seekers to the Other Shore.
May all find happiness through my actions,
and let no one suffer because of me.
Whether they love or hate me,
Whether they hurt or wrong me,
May they all obtain true entrusting,
Through Other Power,
and realize Supreme Nirvana.
Namo Amida Buddha.

During a recent visit to Myanmar, which is known to most people as Burma, I sailed by riverboat on the Irrawaddy River from Mandalay to Yangon (Rangoon), and saw many Buddhist monasteries and temples. I gained some insights into the way Buddhism combines prayer and good deeds in its daily practice. Myanmar has lived under a repressive military regime for decades, and is in the midst of a struggle to democratize and join the community of nations. What is remarkable about the Burmese people living in their towns and villages along the river, most of them making do with modest means, is that for the most part they are content with their lot and have a sunny disposition. They are very devout Buddhists, more so perhaps than most Buddhists I have seen in the rest of Asia. In no other country have I seen more Buddhist temples, pagodas, and stupas, many covered with gold leaf and dominating the landscape along the river. I have seen children and old people crowding those temples and praying with great fervor. I saw a family bring their young son to a monastery to start his studies to become a monk. You could tell the parents were radiating with pride as they were fulfilling what to them was the highest precept of their faith. The boy's younger sister was dressed in a colorful traditional costume, and had her ears pierced in honor of the occasion. She told our guide she was very proud of her brother.

The Buddhist monks in Myanmar play a key role in helping the poor and the needy, while they themselves depend on the charity of the people for their food and sustenance. I saw monks running an orphanage for boys, and I was impressed by the way the older boys took care of the younger ones under the supervision of a monk. During the struggle for democracy in recent years, in which the famous woman dissident Aung San Suu Kyi has played a key role and still does, monks have been martyrized by the military regime and have marched by the thousands in their support for democracy. Indeed, the combined power of prayer and good deeds is very much in evidence this country which has begun to open up to the world.

Real prayer is not a recreational activity. It is not meant to be a "feel good" experience. Like love, prayer is not meant for self-gratification. Love means caring about someone, and caring means being concerned about the wellbeing of the loved one. It also means sacrificing for the one we love. Prayer is meant to be the greatest commitment we can possibly make. It cannot be a half-hearted activity. Jews are commanded to "love Adonai your God with all your heart and with your soul and with all your might." Only when the full meaning of these words enters our hearts, our hearts are ready to pray.

Another form of prayer is what Jews call *talmud torah*, or the study of the Law, and Christians call the study of God's Word. The reading of scriptural passages as part of the service is common to both religions, and it helps enhance the prayers.

But this is not the only study that is a form of prayer. Any kind of study that leads to improving and enriching life is a form of prayer. In the morning service of the traditional Jewish prayer book we find the following meditation:

These are the things for which one enjoys the yield in this world while the principal remains for the world to come:
Honoring father and mother,
Performing deeds of loving kindness,
Punctually attending the house of study morning and evening,
Showing hospitality to guests,
Visiting the sick,

Helping the needy bride,
Attending the dead, praying with devotion,
Making peace among people.
And the study of Torah is equal to all of these.

Why is the study of Torah equal to all of these? Because the Torah, or the law, teaches all of these things, and ensures that they are performed not mechanically but with a knowing heart and an informed mind.

It has been my personal experience on many occasions as I was engaged in study, particularly in the study of Torah, that I felt I was actually praying. I once heard the great British Jewish historian, Cecil Roth, say that he considered study to be a form of prayer. Prayer and knowledge go hand in hand. We pray because we go through life facing the unknown. We do not know what will happen to us next, and we always face what has been referred to as the Great Unknown. Life is a constant search for knowledge, and both praying and studying are a continuous search for answers.

According to the sages of the Talmud, the world stands on three things: Learning, prayer, and good deeds. I submit that all three are one and the same. All three are interdependent, and cannot exist without the other two. To praise God is to be engaged in all three. Some people have a greater ability to study than others, and so they may dedicate more time to study. Others may dedicate more time to prayer. Still others may spend more time helping others. The Jewish view, however, has always been that no one is exempt from doing any one of those three. You study to the extent you are able to, and the same goes for prayer and for acts of love and kindness.

9. PRAYING TO GOD AS A FATHER FIGURE

Jews pray to their "Heavenly Father," and Christians pray to "God the Father." In Judaism, addressing God as father is a metaphor, albeit a very compelling one. In Christianity, God has a son, hence the fatherhood of God for Christians may seem to be quite literal. In Islam, God is not referred to as father. Islam makes a total separation between the human and the divine. It is interesting that Maimonides, the greatest post-Talmudic authority on Jewish belief and practice, who lived in the twelfth century under Islam, makes it clear in his Thirteen Principles of the Faith that God has no bodily image and is not a physical entity. It appears that in the Hebrew Bible God was considered the father of the Jewish people, perhaps a spiritual father, because the children of Abraham, Isaac and Jacob were considered to be the first to discover the one God of the Universe. When God creates Adam, the first human is created "in the image of God," hence the idea that all people are the children of God.

Another male image applied to God in both Jewish and Christian prayer is that of King, Sovereign, Ruler, Lord, as well as "King of Kings." In Christianity the term "King of Kings" is applied to both God the Father and God the Son. Interestingly, the human title of "king" is also applied to God in the Qur'an. Here Muslim scholars have had a problem with this likening of God to a human sovereign. They have tried to explain away this contradiction by arguing that God is the only true king who owns the world, while human kings are God's slaves.

Thus, all the so-called Abrahamic religions believe in God who is the Ruler of the Universe, which, once again, is a dominant male figure. The two images of God as father and as king are combined in the Jewish liturgy of the High Holy days in the words, "*Avinu malkeynu*, our Father our King, we have no king but You."

I have mentioned earlier in discussing the 23rd Psalm that to me God becomes most real as a friend, a teacher, and a guide. God as male authority figure, and particularly as a monarch, raises several questions not only for me but for many other people, particularly for women.

For women the first question is one of gender. Why is God male rather than female? The question of gender in relation to God is not a new one. It appears in all religions since earliest recorded time. With the changing role of women in society in today's world, the question takes on greater urgency.

The standard answer is that God is neither male nor female. God, in other words, has no gender. And yet, images such as father and king are clearly male images. People do not think of God as "it;" they think of God as "He" with a capital H. It is no wonder that on the ceiling of the Sistine Chapel in the Vatican God the Creator is portrayed by Michelangelo as a larger-than-life old man with a flowing white beard. To think of God as a genderless abstraction is something most people find difficult to do.

The other major problem for people living in a democracy is to think of God as a monarch. Having lived in four democracies, I find monarchs to be a thing of the past, certainly not of the present and less so of the future (I must interject, though, that while visiting Oman last year, a well-run Muslim desert country in the Arabian Peninsula, headed by a sultan, the cabdriver told me that monarchy was superior to democracy, since the parliament does not have to quibble over everything, as the sultan takes good care of his people). As for the people of the British Commonwealth, their sovereign is no longer their supreme authority, hence borrowing that title to refer to God seems to be disempowering God.

Here we enter the realm of the language of prayer. Since the Bible was translated into English some four hundred years ago as what has been known as the King James Version, it has been translated innumerable times, and we still see new translations coming out on a regular basis. Language, like religion, evolves, and we no longer use thee's and thou's, nor do we bend the translation as much as we used to in order to make it conform to our beliefs (a good example is the traditional Christian translation of the verse "a maiden is with a child" in Isaiah as "a virgin is with a child," which has been corrected in recent years). The question of the language of prayer is not limited to terms like father and king. It reaches into many other aspects of formal prayer, as we shall see in the chapter about the new language of prayer.

The concepts of God as father and as sovereign are so deeply ingrained in the Scriptures and in the liturgy, that it is hard to know how they can be possibly modified to meet the needs of today's world. Both Christians and Jews are so accustomed to using them that we take them for granted and give them little thought. To take them out of the traditional liturgy would cause the entire traditional prayer edifice to collapse. With this is mind, it should be clear that neither term is to be taken literally. God is "like a father," and God is not a king of flesh and blood, but only a king in the sense that God is the ultimate authority in a universe where man is not.

As for the female figure one addresses in prayer which women may relate to, in some religions, notably in Catholicism, a woman can look up to the Virgin Mary. In Judaism, one does not have a female figure of such rank. The closest Judaism comes in endowing the divinity with a female aspect is the term *shechinah*, which is the presence or indwelling of God, which is feminine. But this is an abstract term which Jewish women do not invoke. Where women in Judaism do find a feminine channel to God, so to speak, is in the intercession of female biblical figures with God, notably the four matriarchs, namely, Sarah, Rebecca, Leah and Rachel. In some recent versions of Jewish prayer books, the names of the matriarchs have been included in the prayers along with the patriarchs.

10. The Kaddish and the Lord's Prayer

While many Jews and even more Christians believe that Jewish prayers and Christian prayers are quite different from each other, mainly because Jews pray directly to God while Christians pray to Jesus, there is much common ground when it comes to the liturgies of both faiths. We have already mentioned the Psalms, which are part of the Hebrew Bible and which are the backbone of both Jewish and Christian prayer. Without the Psalms, attributed to King David, both faiths are stripped of the very essence of their devotion.

But the Psalms are not the only bond between Jewish and Christian prayer. Christian faith is deeply rooted in the saga of the Jewish people as it appears in the Hebrew Bible, beginning with the stories of creation, and reaching its peak with Abraham as the founder of monotheism, and later with Moses as the lawgiver who delivers his people and the world the Ten Commandments, which are the foundation of monotheistic morality. Jesus of Nazareth and his disciples were Jews who prayed as Jews, although they looked for new forms of prayer, which, by the way, was also true of other Jews at that time, such as the Pharisees, who were the founders of Jewish prayer as we know it to this day. For the past sixteen centuries, the majority of the Jewish people have lived in Christian lands, and although both faiths did their best to become separate and different from each other, they have exerted great influence on each other, and still do.

Where Jews and Christians enter a common ground in their life of prayer is in what is perhaps the most important prayer of the Christian world, namely, the Pater Noster, or the Lord's Prayer, which has its origins in the Hebrew prayer known as the Kaddish, perhaps the most important prayer of Judaism.

The alleged origin of the Lord's Prayer could not be more compelling. The story is told in the New Testament (Mat. 6:9-13 and Luke 11:1-4) about the disciples asking Jesus how to prayer:

> And it came to pass, that, as he was praying in a
> certain place, when he ceased, one of his disciples said
> to him, Lord, teach us to pray, as John also taught his
> disciples. And he said to them, when you pray, say,

> Our Father in heaven,
> Hallowed be Your Name.
> Your Kingdom come.
> Your will be done
> on earth As it is in heaven.
> Give us this day our daily bread,
> and forgive our trespasses,
> as we forgive those who trespass against us.
> And lead us not into temptation,
> but deliver us from evil,
> for Yours is the kingdom,
> and the power, and the glory,
> forever and ever.
> Amen.

A Jew who is familiar with the Kaddish prayer immediately notices the similarity between the two prayers in the opening words of the Kaddish:

Magnified and hallowed be God's great name
In the world He created according to His will,
where He establishes His kingdom. . .

The Kaddish goes on:

. . . in your lifetime and during your days,
and within the life of the entire House of Israel,
speedily and soon, and let us say, Amen.

May His great name be blessed forever and to all
eternity.

Blessed and praised, glorified and exalted, extolled
and honored, adored and lauded be the name of the
Holy One, blessed be He, beyond all the blessings and
hymns, praises and consolations that are ever spoken
in the world; and let us say, Amen.

May there be abundant peace from heaven, and life, for
us
and for all Israel; and let us say, Amen.

He who creates peace in His celestial heights, may He
create peace for us and for all Israel; and let us say,
Amen.

In many ways, the Kaddish is the key prayer in Judaism, even as the Lord's Prayer is the key prayer in Christianity. What makes the Kaddish so remarkable is that it is not part of the biblical text, nor is it written in Hebrew, the language of the

Hebrew Bible, but rather in Aramaic, the everyday language in the Near East in the time of Jesus. And yet it became the prayer the Jew recites more often than any other prayer, and serves as the mainstay of the prayer life of the Jew from birth to death. The Lord's Prayer, on the other hand, is attributed directly to Jesus, and therefore has a power all its own no other Christian prayer has.

All my life I have been aware of the power of the Lord's Prayer. A recent Polish film about the massacre of the officer class of the Polish army by the Red Army in World War II at the Katin forest has a scene in which the doomed Polish officers recite the Lord's Prayer. I am constantly haunted by that scene. It shows how a group of them are taken in a covered truck to the forest. When they arrive deep inside the forest, the tailgate of the truck is flung open and the officers are ordered to get off. As they get down they see the Russian soldiers with their submachine guns and the trenches waiting for them. They realize what is about to happen. A group of them begin to recite the Lord's Prayer in deep fervor and resignation. It is the only thing that stands between them and their final hour. As I listened to them pray it was clear to me they were entrusting their lives to God, and that this prayer enabled them to die with dignity.

The same is true of Jews reciting the Kaddish. Many a Jew must have recited the Kaddish as the Nazis lined up Jews along the trenches in Poland and elsewhere in Europe before they massacred them. When the Jew recites the Kaddish, he does the same thing the Christian does when reciting the Lord's Prayer, namely, he sanctifies God's name and accepts God's will in the face of the mystery of human life and death.

One could argue that both prayers are messianic prayers.

Both express the wish that God may establish the "Kingship of God" on earth, which means the beginning of a messianic age, when war and death are no more, and when, in the words of the prophet Isaiah,

The wolf also shall dwell with the lamb,
and the leopard shall lie down with the kid;
and the calf and the young lion
and the fatling together;
and a little child shall lead them.
The wolf will live with the lamb,
and the leopard will lie down with the goat. . .
And lion like the cattle will eat straw.
(11:6-7)

Many would argue that this is an idealized vision which does not take into account the laws of nature. First, most people cannot envision a world without war. And second, the animal kingdom consists of predators and prey. Why, then, would both Judaism and Christianity believe in a world where there is no more war, and no more predators and prey?

Both the Kaddish and the Lord's Prayer envision such a world. Is it possible that someday all carnivorous animals will become herbivorous? Is it possible that someday human nature will change so radically that violence and aggression will be no more?

Both faiths seem to say that it is possible. In the time of Jesus, Jews lived in anticipation of such a world. The world they knew was ruled by the evil empire of Rome. Human life was of little value under Roman rule. Jewish sages like Hillel the Elder, who must have exerted a great influence on the young Jesus, to judge from the similarity of their respective statements about human relations, and later sages like Rabbi Akivah, spoke of a messiah who would come to redeem their people. Jesus brought his disciples a message of such redemption when he said that "the kingdom of heaven was about to come." His disciples believed him to be that redeemer. The belief in a messiah or a messianic age continues to animate both faiths to this day and is best expressed in the Kaddish and in the Lord's Prayer.

11. Magic

For many people today magic is make-believe, something not to be taken seriously. But in the distant and not-so-distant past, magicians were believed to have great powers, and magic was closely related to religion. It is interesting to note that in recent years the public has shown great interest in magic and sorcery, as evidenced by the sales of the Harry Potter novels and by the ongoing stream of science fiction and fantasy movies, all of which require suspension of disbelief and the willingness to be carried away by stories that have little to do with reality.

It is interesting to note that despite the common dismissal of magic, people routinely use the expression, "it is magical," which means, it is *as if* somehow has worked magic. Similarly, people who do not believe in miracles do use the expression "it is miraculous." One would be hard put to find anyone who does not use these two expressions. When it comes to prayer, the ancient element of magic attached to uttering the right words, saying the right prayer, or intoning the right incantation, is still embedded in our minds, no matter how hard we may try to suppress it. I cannot recall how many times people have said to me, "Rabbi, you have a direct channel to God. He will listen to you." What we have here is the need, the desire to believe that a clergyperson today has the magical powers of a Moses, who parted the Red Sea, or Jesus, who could bring the dead back to life.

Once, when I lived in Uruguay in my late teens, I suffered from a persistent fungal infection between my toes, commonly known as athlete's foot. I could not find the right ointment to treat this problem. A housemaid told me that she knew a medicine woman who had the power to get rid of this affliction. It sounded to me like old wives' tale, but since nothing else worked, I decided to give it a try. I went to see that woman, who took me out into her backyard, waved some branches over my foot, and muttered some incantation. As I expected, it failed to have any impact on my condition. The following year I went to the U.S. to go to college, and I was prescribed Desenex antifungal ointment which immediately took care of the problem, and which I continue to use to this day whenever my condition flares up, which has become quite rare.

Throughout time, there has always been a thin line between prayer and magic. There is a captivating story in Jewish lore about a man named Honi the Circler. His title was due to his habit of forcing God to bring down the rain by making a circle on the ground and standing inside the circle and saying to God, I won't move from here until you bring down the rain. Invariably, God would listen to Honi's plea, and the rain would come down. This is an example of prayer as magic. It is interesting that the Talmud, which, in keeping with the teachings of the Bible, does not believe in magic, tells this story with a straight face. As happens in other religions, Judaism has never completely dismissed the ability of righteous or saintly persons to receive God's help in performing a miracle.

Religion, from the time of Abraham to our own time, has always operated on two different levels, namely, formal religion and folk religion. The teachings of formal religion can be found in its sacred texts and its scholarly works. They are based on the high ideals and lofty precepts promulgated by the teachers of that faith. But at the same time, people have always pursued their own folk or even personal beliefs which were easier for them to grasp and which gave them something to hold on to when faced with life's problems. Folk religion includes, among other things, amulets, superstitions, incantations, and, most importantly, magic. When it didn't rain and people's lives depended on a good crop, magic became a handy shortcut to resolving the problem.

A good analogy to the traditional role of magic in folk religion can be found today in gambling. Millions of people gamble or play the lottery, especially those who can least afford it. To me, casinos and lotteries foster and take advantage of this human weakness, and stand in the way of human progress. My friends who go to Las Vegas to gamble do one of two things when they come back—they either tell me they lost "some money," or they claim they won, but their claim more often than not fails to mention that before they won that sum of money, they had lost much more.

The so-called three major Abrahamic religions all decry magic and attribute it to dark powers which are out to snare the innocent and cause harm. And yet, the adherents of all three have a long history which continues to this day of looking for magic to bring protection and prosperity. The *Arabian Nights* are full of stories of spirits and demons and such magical devices as flying carpets and flying horses. Sophisticated or pious Muslims regard these stories as vulgar and look upon them with disdain. But they continue to appear in new editions around the world and they still delight children and adults everywhere.

Among the central characters in the New Testament we

have demons and the master of evil himself, namely, Satan. Until not so long ago, the Christian world has been actively engaged in what is known as witch hunts, not figuratively but literally. So-called witches were burned at the stake throughout the Middle Ages, and executed in colonial America. But despite these harsh measures, people in the Christian world were not willing to give up magic, which was practiced by their ancestors long before they were converted to Christianity.

Jews throughout time have used a variety of amulets and other objects as spiritual symbols that border on magic. An amulet is defined by the dictionary as "an ornament or small piece of jewelry thought to give protection against evil, danger, or disease." Those have included the ornament known as *hamsa*, representing the open palm of a hand with the thumb and the pinkie flaring out like the fronds of a palm tree. This symbol has its origin in ancient Egypt and later in Islam, where it is known as the Hand of Fatima, which includes an eye embedded in the middle of the palm. The *hamsa* became very popular with the Jews of Morocco, who brought it to Israel in the late forties and fifties, where it became once again popular with other Jews as well.

One could argue that the *mezuzah*, a small ornamental box affixed to the doorpost of Jewish homes or places of business, containing a tiny parchment scroll with a biblical text affirming Jewish faith, is also an amulet, which is also worn as a much smaller silver or gold pendant on a necklace by both sexes. Its purpose is "protection against evil, danger, or disease." The same can be said about the phylacteries, or black prayer boxes attached to black leather straps, worn by Orthodox and some traditional Jews on the forehead and on the left arm (the one close to the heart), also containing small scrolls with the relevant text from the Torah, and known in Hebrew as *teffilin*. Both the *mezuzah* and the *teffilin* have their origins in the biblical text which reads,

> *And these words which I command you this day shall be in your heart, and you shall teach them diligently to your children, and shall talk of them when you sit in your house, and when you walk by the way, and when you lie down and rise up. And you shall bind them for a sign upon your hand, and they shall be as frontlets between your eyes. And you shall write them on the doorposts of your house, and on your gates [emphasis added].* (Deut. 6:6-9)

Jews throughout time have believed that the words of the Holy Scriptures and, most particularly, the name of God, have magical powers that can protect them from evil. In biblical times, the proper pronunciation of God's name was only known to the high priest. It consists of four vowels, YHWH, which in English have been rendered as Yaweh or Jehovah, both of which are inaccurate. When Moses first asks God for his name, God replies, "I am who I am," without giving a specific name. God must have revealed His name to Moses' brother Aaron, who became the first high priest, and Aaron's descendants who succeeded him in that role were the custodians of the ineffable name, and were only allowed to pronounce it once a year, on the Day of Atonement, inside the Holy of Holies.

After the destruction of the Temple by the Romans in the year 70 CE, the pronunciation of the name was forgotten. And yet, during the Middle Ages, Jewish mysticism, or Kabbalah, which explores the hidden meaning of the words of Scriptures, claimed that certain sages were able to put the right letters together to produce the *shem ha'meforash*, the revealed name of God. One of the best known examples in that of the holy MAHARAL, Rabbi Judah Loew ben Bezalel of Prague, who looked for a way to protect the Jews of Prague against their enemies. He built a large human figure out of earth and clay, known as a Golem, and wrote the ineffable name on a piece of paper which he inserted in the Golem's mouth, and by saying certain incantations was able to put the breath of life into it. The Golem did the rabbi's bidding as it was called upon to defend the Jews. Here again we have an example of a devout Jew practicing magic, this time in the sixteenth century.

What is remarkable about the Jewish faith is that the Jewish people have a long history of martyrdom, exceeding that of other people. And yet the belief in the protective power of the Holy Writ and the Holy Name continues to this day, especially among the most observant. What seems to emerge here from this comparative look at prayer and magic, is that a process of sublimation has taken place in the past two hundred years, since the time of the Enlightenment, in both Christianity and Judaism, which has created a middle ground between magic and prayer. For the modern Muslim, the Arabian Nights are flights of the imagination, not articles of faith. For the modern Christian, witches are not women endowed with magical powers, but victims of societal ignorance and ill intentions. For the modern Jew, *mezuzot* and *teffilin* are not amulets but ritual objects designed to remind the believer of the sanctity of the text and of life.

Prayer today, like the arts, and like nature itself, seems to contain an element of magic. It is not dark magic, and it is not manipulative magic. It is magic in the suggestive rather than the assertive sense of the word. It is the magic of the human heart, best defined by the great French philosopher Blaise Pascal, "the heart has its reasons of which reason knows nothing." Prayer without magic is like a flower without fragrance. It is to believe in God as a logical syllogism, rather than something one approaches with a sense of "awe and wonder," to use one of the key phrases of the late philosopher of Judaism, Abraham Joshua Heschel. In a positive, constructive way, life is full of magic. We see it every day in the rising and the setting of the sun; in the smile of a child; in someone extending a helping hand to a stranger; in people beaten down by the harshness of existence, and pulling themselves up, standing up, squaring their shoulders, and starting over again. Prayer is, indeed, about the magic of man's limitless capacity for good; the indomitable spirit that has taken man to the moon and beyond, that has allowed man to cure seemingly incurable diseases; to communicate across oceans and continents; to turn deserts into blooming gardens; and to articulate immortal words such as, "It has been told you, O man, what is good, and what your God asks of you, but to do justice, and love mercy, and walk humbly with your God."

But prayer is not wizardry, and it is not about gambling. Incantation does not replace proactive faith, and gambling is not a shortcut to prosperity. Prayer, like religion itself, can be easily misused and abused. As the Hebrew Bible amply demonstrates, these things were clearly understood by the ancient Hebrews, who lived in a world steeped in magic, superstitions, and ignorance. Surrounded by nations who worshipped idols and whose priests performed magic, the biblical Hebrews grasped the limitations of human beings, and understood that there is a higher force worth praying to, and that this higher force expects man to do the heavy lifting. Out of this conviction they gave the world prayer and ethical teachings which have impacted all the major religions and all cultures to this day.

12. SACRIFICE

Before there was prayer, there was sacrifice. In Judaism, animal sacrifices ceased at the time of the destruction of the Jerusalem Temple, where animal sacrifices were offered. This coincides with the time of the birth of Christianity, a faith which regards the sacrifice of the Christian Savior as the ultimate sacrifice that brought redemption to the world. Judaism replaced sacrifices with prayer, a radical, revolutionary change in the long history of Jewish worship. The rabbis at the time, who sought to justify such a radical change, used a quote from the Book of Hosea, which said, "Take with you words, and return unto Adonai; say to Him: 'Forgive all iniquity, and accept that which is good; so will we render for bullocks the offering of our lips." (14:3)

This was not only a bold move, but also one that remained controversial to this day. Judaism has never disavowed completely the ritual of sacrifices. Many Orthodox Jews today believe that the Holy Temple will be rebuilt someday, and the sacrificial cult will be restored. In Talmudic academies the devout continue to study the laws of the sacrifices in anticipation of such a time.

From the beginning of time, humans have felt the need to gain favor from the mysterious powers of the universe by making offerings of different kinds. This practice is played out in the story of Cain and Abel, who bring God offerings from their work:

> *Abel tended his sheep, while Cain was a tiller of the ground. And in the course of time it happened that Cain brought of the fruit of the ground an offering to*

God. And Abel brought of the firstlings of his flock and of the fat thereof. (Gen. 4:2-4)

Here the shepherd offers sheep, while the farmer offers the fruit of his harvest. One may wonder: why would a supernatural being need sheep and produce? Quite clearly, going back to prehistoric times, the concept of a non-corporeal god did not exist. In all ancient mythologies, the gods go hungry and need to be fed. Since the gods do not tend livestock and do not till the soil, it becomes the responsibility of humans to provide them with food.

Besides feeding the gods, sacrifices were also used to feed the priestly class, which did not raise food either. But the main purpose of offering animal sacrifices for the person making the offering was to atone for a sin by transferring the guilt to the sacrificial animal and offering its life in place of the sinner's life. The best example of this practice was the sacrifice of the goat on the Day of Atonement as part of the Jerusalem temple ritual designed to atone all the sins of Israel, when a goat was sent into the desert carrying all those sins (hence the term "scapegoat").

As the idea of a non-physical god begins to take hold in Judaism as well as in Christianity and later in Islam, sacrifices are no longer practiced by the followers of those religions. Now food becomes sacramental and symbolic, as in the case of the wafer and the wine representing the flesh and blood of Christ. In Eastern religions, such as Buddhism, offerings of food are still brought today to the temple or the shrine as part of the prayer and meditation ritual. Blessings are intoned over food in Judaism as a way of thanking God for bringing forth food from the earth.

Prayer and food are closely linked in all faith systems. Many houses of worship today collect food for the poor, as one of the most important precepts of religion is to feed the hungry.

Another form of sacrifice designed to appease and please the gods has been human sacrifice. In the Bible, the judge Jephthah sacrifices his daughter after returning victorious from the battlefield. In Greek mythology, King Agamemnon sacrifices his daughter Iphigenia for a similar reason. Throughout time, human sacrifice was practiced by ancient civilizations like the Aztecs and the Mayans who sought to please their gods by sacrificing their enemies. The list of human sacrifice practices is long indeed.

One could argue that since the beginning of organized warfare between tribes and nations, soldiers have been sacrificed to protect their people, a practice that continues today throughout the world. One could further argue that atrocities committed by political and religious fanatics from Nazis to Islamist terrorists are also a form of human sacrifice.

But at the same time, the concept of sacrifice is deeply ingrained in human reality. In times of crisis, such as national emergencies, economic collapse, drought, epidemic, and so on, people are called upon to make sacrifices. A person who looks to achieve an important goal must be prepared to make sacrifices. In other words, prayer has not taken the place of sacrifices, but rather has been introduced into people's lives as a way of reflecting on the nature of life and the relation between the human and the divine, which calls upon each person to be prepared to makes sacrifices to improve one's life and contribute to the common welfare.

A story of sacrifice as a supreme example of brotherly love has appeared in Jewish sources and merits to be mentioned here:

Long before the Holy Temple was built on Mount Moriah in Jerusalem, two brothers lived and farmed on that site. One was married and had a large family, while the other was single. They lived in close proximity to each other, and each worked his land growing wheat. When harvest time arrived, each was blessed with a bountiful crop and piled up his grain for long-term storage.

The unmarried brother, observing his good fortune, thought to himself that God had blessed him with more than he needed, whereas his brother, who was blessed with a large family, could surely use more. He arose in the middle of the night and secretly took from his grain and put it in his brother's pile.

Similarly, the married brother thought to himself that he was fortunate to have children who will care for him in his old age, while his brother will depend on what he saved. He, too, arose in the middle of the night and quietly transferred grain from his pile to his brother's.

In the morning, each brother wondered why there was no noticeable decrease in his own pile, and so they repeated the transfer the next night. These nocturnal activities went on for several nights, until one night the brothers bumped into each other. In that instant, in the dark of night, they each understood what the other had been doing and fell into each other's arms in a loving embrace. According to legend, when God saw that display of brotherly love He selected the site for His future Temple.

13. PRAYER, WORK, AND CREATIVITY

Some people pray with their hands, and some people pray with their creative imagination. By that I mean that someone who plant a tree, or someone who paints a landscape, is also praying. The Psalmist says: "The earth is the Lord's, and the fullness thereof." (24:1) Planting a tree is helping God with the ongoing work of creation. It is a creative and redemptive act. We have already mentioned the story about Honi the Circler, who forced God to bring down the rain. The story goes on to tell us how one day Honi saw an old man planting a cherub tree, which takes seventy years to bear fruit. Do you expect to enjoy the fruit of this tree? Honi asked. No, said the old man. I am planting it so that my children's children may enjoy it. Planting that tree was a form of prayer.

Two of the greatest artists of all time, Van Gogh and Gauguin, while at odds with the church, were each in his own way deeply religious and spiritual people. They were not exactly saintly people, but they were what has been described as "God-intoxicated people." Van Gogh's early aspiration was to become a pastor. But painting became his all-consuming passion, and many of his canvasses, such as *The Sower*, convey deep religious faith. Gauguin, in several of his works, paints himself as a representation of Christ. Art and religious faith have been going hand in hand since the beginning of time. While both Judaism and Islam forbid human imagery in depicting the divine, because originally it was closely associated with paganism, Christian Europe, continuing the artistic traditions of Greece and Rome, created many of the world's best known works of art as a means of enhancing religious faith. Many of the great masterpieces of the Renaissance have religious themes. Michelangelo's *Pietà*, and Leonardo de Vinci's *Virgin of the Rocks* are among the better known.

There is something spiritual about all genuine art (as opposed to art with an ulterior motive, such as commercialism, self-aggrandizement, or propaganda). This applies to all forms of art, not only visual. For the past two centuries, many artists—painters, poets, playwrights, and others—have been taking sides in a debate about "art for art's sake," which argues that art needs no other reason than its own artistic expression. In other words, art does not have a social or moral purpose; its sole purpose is to create something beautiful which people may enjoy. The chief or only aim of a work of art is the self-expression of the individual artist who creates it.

Two famous Irishmen who took opposite sides in this debate were Oscar Wilde and George Bernard Shaw. Wilde was a defender of art for art's sake. He saw the artist as a rebel against society, who only answered to his own calling. An opponent of this theory was George Bernard Shaw, who maintained that art had a social and a moral purpose, without which it was of no value. It seems to me that there is a spiritual dimension to both of their opposite approaches. In denouncing the ills of society from their different perspectives, Wilde, the individualist, affirmed the role of the artist as one who imitates God in creating a work of art that helps people better understand themselves and the world around them. The worth of each individual person is affirmed by the Talmudic saying, "Every person must say, the world was created for my sake." In other words, every person is a world unto themselves. Shaw, the socialist, on the other hand, affirms the purpose of art as a vehicle to improve both the individual and society. Both of these great dramatists had a valid point of view. Moreover, both had a remarkable gift of humor that has helped us laugh at ourselves and gain a more benign view of life.

Not every person is a creative genius, nor is everyone expected to be one. But most people are endowed with intelligence and energy which can be put to good use. The ancient Greeks had a saying which became very popular in the United States: "God helps those who help themselves." To me, truer words were never spoken. Prayer is good and well, but without action it is of no use. When we ask God for help, I can hear God saying, have you done everything you can to help yourself? If not, don't expect me to do it for you.

Since ancient times, Judaism has put great emphasis on work. In fact, the traditional term for prayer in Judaism is *avodah*, work, or *avodat ha'kodesh*, holy work. Idol worshiping, on the other hand, is called *avodat elilim*, or idol work. Thus, work and prayer from early on have been considered in Jewish thought to be one and the same. Prayer does not exist by itself or in and of itself. It is an integral part of living a productive life and acting as partner with God in the work of creation. To receive help from the Almighty, man must take responsibility as a partner, not a passive bystander.

Many people approach prayer with a passive attitude. When they walk into their house of worship they are awed by the mystery of the place and they go through the motions of the ritual without putting their heart and their mind into it. They give little thought to the words of the prayer book, and many do not understand what those words are trying to convey. They are not "working" at praying, but rather letting themselves be carried along by the sound and rhythm of the seemingly familiar text which they have gone through many times before without ever meditating on its meaning or questioning its relevance to their own life and experience. Even those who read the prayers out loud and sing with feeling, do not necessarily understand and feel what they are saying or singing. Their heart may be in the right place, and their fervor is real, but it has little to do with what the words are saying, because they have never taken the time to delve into the meaning and the possibilities of those words. A key prayer in the Jewish liturgy is the *ve'haavta*, or "you shall love the Lord your God," which follows the *sh'ma*, "Hear O Israel." It says:

> *And you shall teach them diligently to your children,*
> *and you shall speak of them when you sit in your house*
> *and when you walk by the way, and when you lie down*
> *and when you rise up.*

How many Jews today when they recite this prayer think about their obligation to impart the knowledge and values of Judaism to their children? How many realize that this is the only way for Judaism to survive? In other words, how many realize how critical these words are to a Jew?

I am asking a rhetorical question, because I know the answer: not too many. I cannot think of a better example where the words of the prayer book, taken directly from the Torah, have lost their meaning for so many.

Praying can be hard work. The transition from the material world to the world of the spirit is not always easy.

One thing Hasidic Jews are taught to do is spend up to an hour preparing themselves mentally and spiritually for prayer. You often see Hasidic Jews prior to praying closing their eyes, swaying back and forth, humming a tune, and gathering their thoughts. What they are doing is engaging in what is known as *kavanah*. This term, which is hard to translate, means concentrating, putting aside all extraneous thoughts and feelings, and focusing on the object of one's prayer. It means leaving the physical world behind, and entering the world of the spirit. It means softening one's heart and opening up to the plenitude of God's presence in the world. It leads to *d'vekut*, or clinging to the divine, and it culminates in *hitlahavut*, an emotional upsurge bordering on ecstasy.

14. MEDITATION

To pray is to address a higher power, such as God. To meditate is to address one's inner self. Addressing one's inner self may lead to addressing God, or it may lead to finding inner strength which may or may not involve God. Prayer today is associated mainly with organized religion, while meditation is more of a personal activity. It takes on many different forms, and it can be found in all cultures and in all faiths. Every human being, believer and nonbeliever, has an inner life. Man is a thinking animal, and meditation is a universal human activity.

Since the sixties and the seventies of the last century, there has been a wide-spread disillusionment with the ability of Western religions and their liturgies to provide answers for today's spiritual and emotional needs, and such meditative activities as yoga, transcendental meditation, Zen meditation, Tao meditation, and many other forms of meditation, including those of Muslim Sufism, Jewish Kabbalah, and other types of meditative mysticisms, have attracted many followers in the West.

Meditation is at the heart of Eastern religions. While prayer addresses an external supreme being, meditation is a turning inwardly and finding that being inside oneself. This is particularly true of Buddhism, where the Buddha is not exactly a supreme being but rather the ideal person who had reached the highest level of human development, and has become a model for his followers who strive to become "buddhas" like him. Other Eastern religions—Hinduism, Jainism, Sikhism, Taoism, Confucianism, Shinto and their many offshoots have their own forms and techniques of meditation.

One may argue that Buddhism begins and ends with meditation. Meditative prayer is taught to Buddhist children at a young age, and the ultimate goal of life according to Buddhist teachings is nirvana, which is defined as a transcendent state in which there is neither suffering, desire, nor sense of self, and the subject is released from the effects of karma and the cycle of death and rebirth. It represents the final goal of Buddhism. This, in effect is the perfect meditative state, which also characterizes the state of the blessed dead in the afterlife according to the three monotheistic religions.

This definition of nirvana contains several key concepts of Buddhism which have become widely familiar in the West, such as karma and the "cycle of birth and death." Karma is defined as "the sum of a person's actions in this and previous states of existence, viewed as deciding their fate in future existences." It implies the Buddhist belief in reincarnation, which is defined as the religious or philosophical concept that the soul or spirit, after biological death, can begin a new life in a new body. This doctrine is a central tenet of the Indian religions.

The basic premise of meditation in Buddhism and in other Eastern religions is that while many things that happen to us in this life are beyond our control, we do have control over our mind, and through certain exercises and thought processes we can modify our state of mind and overcome negative feelings such as anger, anxiety and fear. Then we can achieve a state of wellbeing and serenity, which enables us to look at life more calmly and compassionately, and reach a higher state of being.

For years I have had difficulties with the Buddhist concept of reincarnation. The thought of coming back from the netherworld in the form of a frog or a beetle seemed too fanciful. But as I got older I began to discern some deep spirituality in this concept. I take this belief to mean that all of life is interrelated: human, animal, and perhaps even plant. Buddhists treat all living creatures with much more compassion that we do in the West. Overall, they seem to be gentler and kinder people than we are. Now that I have grandchildren, I notice that a particular grandchild reminds me of one of my parents and grandparents. People do not exist in isolation but are rather interrelated. They live on in the life of their descendants and, who knows, their life may extend even beyond family members and fellow humans. I have not espoused the Buddhist belief in reincarnation, but I have learned to respect it.

Many argue that Buddhism and other Eastern religions are not actually religions in the Western sense of the word but rather philosophies or ways of life. As such, they allow us to partake of their wisdom without expecting us to give up our original beliefs. I am perfectly comfortable to be a Jew who practices Buddhist meditation, because, unlike a Buddhist, I do not nor am I expected to become a Buddha. Here again we see how Eastern religions are more accepting of outsiders than we are. And, indeed, the great gift of those religions to the West in our time is their rich experience with meditation.

But meditation is not the exclusive domain of Eastern religions. It exists in all other religions and cultures as well. In Judaism, the founders of the Jewish faith from Abraham to Moses found God through meditation, not through prayer.

Abraham does not turn to God in prayer; rather God turns to Abraham and tells him,

Go forth from your country where you were born
and from your parents' house and go the land
which I will show you. (Gen. 12:1)

Abraham discovers the voice of God within himself. He listens to his heart and he finds a channel inside himself that enables him to receive ongoing messages from an otherworldly source, which results in the greatest revolution in all of human history, viz., the birth of monotheism. The same is true of his son, Isaac, and his grandson, Jacob. When Jacob runs away from his brother Esau, he lies down to sleep in the field and he hears God speak to him in a dream. Here again it is the meditative process that makes Jacob hear the voice of God.

It is important to point out that both Abraham and Jacob find God in solitude, which is one of the main characteristics of meditation. The same is true of Moses who, four hundred years later, will rediscover Abraham's God, who does not appear to him in Egypt, but in the solitude of the Sinai Desert, where Moses is tending the flock of his father in law, Jethro. While looking at a bush that is burning but is not consumed.* As Moses is looking at this seemingly inexplicable sight, he begins to commune with the divine,

---

A natural phenomenon that actually happens to this day in the Sinai Desert, where hardy, oily little bushes can catch fire in the intense heat of summer. The fire dies out while the plant remains and is able to regenerate.

and his mission to liberate his people from Egyptian bondage is communicated to him.

Moses, the Father of the Prophets, will give rise in time to generations of Hebrew prophets, from Samuel to Malachi, who will continue the Abrahamic and Mosaic tradition of finding God in solitude and meditation. Foremost among them is Elijah, who runs away from King Ahab to the desert, and witnesses a great storm at the end of which he hears a "still small voice," and is told about his mission. The great prophets of Israel, from Amos to Ezekiel, who have left us a written record of their prophecies, were all solitary people whose communing with God was a meditative, rather than a praying process.

Two major movements in Judaism, one dating back to Mishnaic and medieval times and the other to the eighteenth century, also put a great emphasis on meditation. The first was the mystic tradition in Judaism, which dates back to such sages as Rabbi Shimon bar Yohai (2nd century CE), and culminates centuries later in the work of the great Kabbalists, notably Rabbi Isaac Luria, the Holy Ari, the 16th century mystic who is considered the father of contemporary Kabbalah. Meditative Kabbalah which is usually reserved for the most pious Jews is a solitary way of communing with the divine and at times achieving the power of influencing God's will, more so than can be done through prayer.

In the early Eighteenth century, what is known today as the Hasidic movement in Judaism, was founded by a country mystic and healer named Rabbi Israel, or the Besht (acronym of "He of the Good Name.") Rabbi Israel was a solitary, meditative person who applied Kabbalistic teaching to the Jewish life of prayer and piety, known as "practical

Kabbalah." To this day, his followers in the various Hasidic movements practice what is in effect meditative prayer. We have mentioned the way Hasidim prepare for prayer by first going through a long process of meditating and reaching the point where the prayer becomes a deep emotional and spiritual experience.

To this day, all of Jewish liturgy is a blend between formal prayers and silent meditation, in which the spoken prayer is a communal experience, while the meditation is a solitary personal experience.

In the Christian prayer experience, meditation or, more formally, contemplation, has been the domain mainly of those who dedicate their life to God, such as monks and nuns. Elsewhere in this book we discuss the Trappist monk Thomas Merton who dedicated his life to meditation, and whose writings have had a great impact on post-World War II Christian life. Another example of the contemplative life is St. Teresa de Avila (1515 –1582) of Spain, whose mystical experience has made her one of the best known and influential Christian contemplatives.

The Christian contemplative experience begins with stories of Jesus in the New Testament. When we first hear Jesus refer to prayer in the text following the Sermon on the Mount, he says,

> *But when you pray, go to your private room, shut yourself in, and so pray to your Father who is in that secret place, and your Father who sees all that is done in secret will reward you. (Matt 6:6)*

This passage is clearly open to interpretation, but what the founder of the new religion seems to imply is that the highest form of communing with God is solitary meditation, rather than communal prayer which Pharisaic Judaism at that time emphasized and what normative Judaism still emphasizes to this day. For Judaism, as is the case with Islam, prayer is a means to unify the community of the faithful, following the rule of *vox populi est vox dei*, or the unified voice of the people is where God is to be found. This has led to the rabbinic rule that a *minyan*, or a quorum of at least ten men is required to have a full prayer service. What we see in the case of the man who gave rise to the Christian faith, is a return to biblical prophetic Judaism when solitary meditation was the preferred way to communicate with the divine, rather than spoken prayer.

As Christianity grew and became the dominant religion of the West and eventually of the entire world, communal prayer became as important as it is in all major religions. But the role of contemplatives like St. Teresa or Thomas Merton in serving as models of deep faith and communing with the divine has been extremely important.

The Catholic Church speaks of "mental prayer," which is recommended as a way of cultivating love of God through dialogue by meditating on God's words and contemplating God's face, an idea dating back to the Hebrew Bible. The meditating person envisions God's presence and appearance and enters a state of devotion to God. This is different from what the Church calls "vocal prayer," which is the reciting of printed text, albeit mental prayer can also involve vocal prayer in the process of enhancing the dialogue with God. Here again St. Teresa was one of the leading exponents of mental prayer. She defined it as a "close interaction between friends. . . taking time to be alone with the one we know loves us" (*Las moradas*, 141). Her use of the word "friends" in describing her relationship to God fits well with what I have described here as my own personal relationship with God, toward whom I feel friendship rather than fear.

The *Catechism of the Catholic Church* considers meditation and contemplative prayer which take place in mental prayer as major expressions of the life of prayer. What is the difference between meditation and contemplation? The two terms seem to be identical. When we meditate or when we contemplate we are engaged in a mental process of assessing something in our mind. And yet in the teachings of St. Teresa and other Catholic contemplatives there is a basic difference between the two. Meditation is a process one initiates to achieve a level of faith, also known as clinging to God. It may also involve prayer and other activities, and, as explained by St. Teresa, it involves a progression of several stages of faith. Contemplation, on the other hand, is a state one reaches in which it is no longer the person who is seeking God, but rather God who responds to the meditate efforts of that person and opens up to him or her, so to speak, with what the mystics call the plenitude or fullness of God's presence. Apparently, this can happen to any person, but it is most likely to happen to someone who is actively involved in the life of prayer and meditation.

15. HUMILITY

We read in the Bible that "The man Moses was exceedingly humble, more than any person on the face of the earth" (Numbers 12:3). The Bible does not discuss any of Moses' other character traits. It only tells us that he was humble. We find the same trait of humility in other key biblical characters, such as Jeremiah, who is called upon by God to become a prophet, but responds that he is only a lad and he is not up to the task; or Isaiah who, when called upon to prophesy, says, "Woe is me! For I am undone; because I am a man of unclean lips, and I dwell in the midst of a people of unclean lips: for mine eyes have seen the King, the God of hosts" (6:5). The major theme that runs through the Book of Isaiah is man's pride, the opposite trait of humility. Pride, according to Isaiah, is man's undoing.

The Hebrew prophet who summarized humility in one phrase that has remained one of the key expressions of prophetic Judaism is the prophet Micah, who says:

> *Now it has been told to you O man what is good,*
> *And what Adonai your God demands of you:*
> *But to do justice, and love mercy,*
> *And walk humbly with Adonai your God. (6:8)*

Here indeed are words to live by!

The idea of humility as the true measure of a person of faith runs through all the major religions. Mother Teresa, the world-renowned Roman Catholic nun, had the following to say about humility:

These are the few ways we can practice humility:
To speak as little as possible of one's self.
To mind one's own business.
Not to want to manage other people's affairs.
To avoid curiosity.
To accept contradictions and correction cheerfully.
To pass over the mistakes of others.
To accept insults and injuries.
To accept being slighted, forgotten and disliked.
To be kind and gentle even under provocation.
Never to stand on one's dignity.
To choose always the hardest.
(Mother Teresa, The Joy in Loving: A Guide to Daily Living)

The key concept in Islam is humble surrender to God. The believing Muslim in his daily prayers prostrates himself before God as a profound expression of humility. Here are two Muslim comments on this aspect of Islam:

Successful indeed are the believers, those who humble themselves in their prayers. . . (Al-Muminoon 23:1-2)

Has not the time arrived for the believers that their hearts in all humility should engage in the remembrance of Allah and of the Truth which has been revealed to them. . . (Al-Hadid 57:16)

To pray is to humble oneself before God. One is called upon to love God, and also to see God as a caring friend, but above all else one is expected to always be cognizant of all that God is and man is not. When the twentieth century Hebrew novelist Shmuel Yosef Agnon received a call from the Swedish Royal Academy that he was awarded the Nobel Prize in literature, he sat at his small desk and wrote a note to himself, quoting from the story of Adam and Eve in the Book of Genesis: "For you are dust, and to dust you will return." (3:19) Agnon, the greatest Hebrew novelist of modern times, was a shy and unassuming man.

When the founder of the State of Israel, David Ben-Gurion, called Albert Einstein and asked him to become the first president of the Jewish state, Einstein declined, saying he lacked "the natural aptitude and the experience to deal properly with people."

In my recent visit to Myanmar, formerly Burma, the most devout Buddhist country in Asia, I came face to face with the humility of Buddhism. Like Christian monks, Buddhist monks also live the life of poverty, but go a step further in that they have to beg for food. At the same time, they dedicate their lives to helping others, educating the young and helping the sick and the needy. Prayer is a constant in the lives of the Burmese people, whom I found praying in their temples all the way from Mandalay to Yangon. All the teachings of the Buddha are based on humility, on learning how to accept the limitations of human life, and through seeking enlightenment to strive to reach a higher state of being.

In the Bible, King Solomon was called "the wisest of men." The problem with Solomon was that, unlike Moses, he was not the humblest of men. He lived a life of luxury, took many wives, and had many horses, all of which was prohibited to a Hebrew king, as explained in the Five Books of Moses. And so Solomon was punished by God, in that his kingdom was split in two, and went into decline. His father, David, was a more controversial king than the son, but David knew how to humble himself before god, and while he was punished for taking Bathsheba from her husband by having the son she bore him die at birth, he was able to mend his ways and was granted forgiveness. His people also forgave him, and credited him with the authorship of the Book of Psalms and the fathering of the messiah.

One of the most beautiful sayings I have ever heard, which is attributed to Abraham Lincoln, but which I believe I heard stated by the Big Brother organization, is: "No one stands so tall as when he stoops to help a child." Humility is the bridge between good deeds and prayer. Prayer without good deeds is useless, and good deeds can only be enhanced by prayer. Put differently, prayer which does not lead to good deeds is not real prayer. To quote the Psalms again:

> *Who shall ascend the mountain of Adonai,*
> *And who shall stand in His Holy place?*
> *He who has clean hands and a pure heart,*
> *Who has not taken My name in vain*
> *And has not sworn deceitfully. (24:3-4)*

Only through humility can one achieve the state of "clean hands and a pure heart." The flipside of humility is arrogance, pride, and self-aggrandizing. Those qualities have no place in the life of prayer. This has been clear to every faith system that has endured throughout time.

16. TRIUMPHALISM

All the three monotheistic faiths, whether intentionally or unintentionally, have suffered from triumphalism, which is reflected in either their liturgies or in their teaching and preaching. Triumphalism is the notion that one has a monopoly on God, that one's religion is the only valid one, and that everyone else lives in error. This attitude has brought the world much strife and trouble, and has resulted in the spilling of much innocent blood.

The worst example of triumphalism in the early part of the twenty-first century is radical Islam. On September 11, 2001, now known as 9/11, nineteen militants associated with the Islamic extremist group al-Qaeda hijacked four airliners and carried out suicide attacks against targets in the United States. Two of the planes were flown into the towers of the World Trade Center in New York City; a third plane hit the Pentagon just outside Washington, D.C.; and the fourth plane crashed in a field in Pennsylvania because of intervention by two brave passengers. The attacks resulted in extensive death and destruction, triggering major U.S. initiatives to combat terrorism and defining the presidency of George W. Bush. Over 3,000 people were killed during the attacks in New York City and Washington, D.C., including more than 400 police officers and firefighters.

This was the defining moment for radical Islam, but by no means the only one. The radical Islam monster has many heads, like the water monster Hydra in Greek mythology which, when one head is cut off, two new ones grow in its place. As of this writing, radical Islam is represented by countries like Iran, and by terrorist organizations like ISIS,

Al Shabaab, Hezbollah, Hamas, and more. In the name of Islam claiming to be the only true faith, the Middle East is being depleted of its Christian populations, some of which have been living there for centuries; innocent people from Syria to Nigeria are being murdered in cold blood; and millions of people, mostly Muslims, have been displaced. These atrocities, whether intentionally or coincidentally, are reminiscent of the darkest ages in human history.

Islam is not a violent faith, nor are the vast majority of Muslims in today's world violent people. Islamic states experienced golden ages in Baghdad, Constantinople, and in Spain, when Christian Europe was going through the Dark Ages. Islam gave the world algebra and astronomy, medicine and philosophy. Eventually Christian Europe, starting with the era of the Crusades in the Middle Ages, eclipsed the Muslim empires or caliphates, and Muslim civilization went into decline, the results of which can be seen to this day.

There has been much debate in recent years whether humanity is going through a clash of civilizations between the Christian and the Muslim worlds. There is certainly no war going on similar to the two world wars of the twentieth century. But worldwide terrorist attacks by radical Islamists, and the unprecedented increase in Muslim populations throughout the Christian world continue to present great challenges to countries from Spain to Sweden and from Canada to Argentina.

In the United States there has been in recent years a great drive for religious ecumenism, which has been aimed at bringing the six million Muslims living in the U.S. into the mainstream. It is too early to gauge the results. Certainly 9/11 made many Americans feel that Muslims do not have the best interest of the U.S. at heart, resulting in a great deal of prejudice and animosity against them. But it seems that with the latest atrocities committed by ISIS and with the encroachment of the radical regime in Iran throughout the Middle East, countries like Saudi Arabia, Jordan, Egypt and the Emirates have begun to take action against the terrorists and the Arab Middle East has entered a new phase in its search for stability and change for the better in this part of the world.

As was stated earlier, all religions evolve and adjust themselves to changing conditions and views. One major problem in the Muslim world seems to be that there has been little evolution in the liturgy and beliefs of Islam. One major example is the role of women in the Muslim world. While Christianity and Judaism have seen a sea change in our time in the status of women (for example, the ordination of women in the Episcopalian Church and in Reform and Conservative Judaism), in conservative Islamic nations change is still far off. Much of the Muslim world suffers from economic and political stagnation for several reasons, one of which is the failure to utilize the full potential of half of its human population.

In recent years I have visited some of the major mosques in the Arab world, in places like Casablanca, Morocco; Istanbul, Turkey; Cairo, Egypt; and Abu Dhabi, United Arab Emirates. I did not experience any attitudes of triumphalism. On the contrary, I was impressed by the simplicity and dignity of those mega-mosques which accommodate thousands of worshippers. I found the ablutions before prayer to be a sign of great respect for the faith, and the prayers themselves to be soulful and sincere. It was indeed an act of submission to a higher force, which is what the word "islam" means.

The Catholic Church may be the religious body that has seen the most significant change in triumphalism than any other in recent years. The adjective "catholic" means universal. The Catholic Church has always believed itself to be the universal church of the human race, with humanity divided between those who practice Catholicism and those who someday will "see the light" and come around to the "true faith." I once asked a Jesuit friend why the Catholic Church in the U.S. was so concerned about, say, Jewish women having an abortion. He explained that the Church considers itself responsible for the souls of all women, and therefore takes a "catholic," or universal stand on this and other issues.

Catholic triumphalism changed radically with Vatican II, or the Second Vatican Council, which formally opened under the pontificate of Pope John XXIII on October 11, 1962 and closed under Pope Paul VI on the Feast of the Immaculate Conception in 1965. One of its most sweeping statements relates to Jews and Judaism:

> *True, the Jewish authorities and those who followed their lead pressed for the death of Christ; still, what happened in His passion cannot be charged against all the Jews, without distinction, then alive, nor against the Jews of today. Although the Church is the new people of God, the Jews should not be presented as rejected or accursed by God, as if this followed from the Holy Scriptures [emphasis added]. All should see to it, then, that in catechetical work or in the preaching of the word of God they do not teach anything that*

does not conform to the truth of the Gospel and the spirit of Christ. Furthermore, in her rejection of every persecution against any man, the Church, mindful of the patrimony she shares with the Jews and moved not by political reasons but by the Gospel's spiritual love, decries hatred, persecutions, displays of anti-Semitism, directed against Jews at any time and by anyone.

With this statement the Church did away with twenty centuries of dubbing the Jews "Christ Killers" and Judaism a rejected religion. Not that anti-Semitism suddenly disappeared—far from it. Hatemongering is alive and well in today's world. But finally, at long last, the feet were cut from under one of the most malicious canards the world has ever known, and a new day began in Christian-Jewish relations.

This brings us to Jewish triumphalism. Judaism has never spread around the world in numbers nearly as vast as Christianity and Islam. The Jews of the world can be put in one small corner of either the Christian or the Muslim world and not even be noticed. And yet, Jews are one of the best known minorities of the world. They also have the distinction of being the parent religion of both of those world religions. A reading of the New Testament and the Quran shows clearly the origin of the two religions. The prophets of Israel are revered by both. It is remarkable that when God tells Abraham to leave his home and go to a land God would show him, he is told that "all the families of the earth will be blessed through you" (Gen 12:3), as indeed happens many centuries later.

But here is where we run into problems. In Deuteronomy 10:15 we read: "Yet God set his affection on your ancestors and loved them, and he chose you, their descendants, above all the nations—as it is today." Thus, from the very beginning of Israel's existence, those desert nomads who conquered the Land of Canaan, also known as the Promised Land, were told that they were God's chosen. Looking back across the centuries, it was not such a great good fortune to be chosen. Jewish history is not exactly a joyride. But worst of all, the idea of chosenness was misunderstood by the world, which took it to mean that Jews consider themselves superior to others, when in reality it meant that they were picked for a most difficult task, that of bearing witness to the world of the one God of all humanity, and of God's law of justice and mercy.

It can be argued that indeed the Jews themselves misunderstood their mission by developing a triumphalist attitude in their liturgy, which makes several references to being God's favorites, hence better than others. This is not so hard to understand when we consider the fact that for some two thousand years the Jews were a small persecuted minority, and it is in the nature of vulnerable minorities to spin a yarn about being superior to others and suffering for it.

In the chapter which discusses a new language of prayer we will take a look at those prayers, and make some suggestions on how to bring them into better harmony with today's world.

17. SIN

We are told "it's a sin to tell a lie." We are also told that something is "sinfully good." The truth is, while the meaning of this little word seems so obvious, it is not obvious at all. My search for the meaning of sin as understood by the various world religions resulted in more confusion than enlightenment. It seems to me that over time people have managed to weigh this word down with such a heavy load of connotations and interpretations that it no longer stands for anything people can readily relate to in today's world.

In colonial America people were frightened by the word sin. Sin was the weapon preachers wielded to keep their people in line. Sinners could expect to be punished for their sins by burning with "fire and brimstone," and enduring the horrific agony of hell for all eternity. Even today, there are those radical fundamentalist groups who continue to hold such extreme beliefs.

But for the most part, sin ain't what it used to be. It has been soft-pedaled by psychologists and social scientists and by the rejection of radical religion by most people. This, perhaps, has made the confusion of what sin is all about even greater, and yet, the concept of sin, such as it is, is still one of the key concepts in most liturgies. Within both Judaism and Christianity, sin still runs the gamut from the Catholic concept of the "original sin" committed by Adam and Eve, which causes every newly born, Jew and Gentile, to be born in sin, to the understanding of the Hebrew word "sin" as a derivation from the verb "to miss the mark," thus making sin more of an error than a willful violation of a divine command.

The three so-called Abrahamic religions have identified

a hierarchy of sins, ranging from the lightest to the gravest. At the bottom of the list are sins that cause little harm to the one who commits them or to others, and therefore can be easily rectified. At the top of the list are sins which are so grave that there is no forgiveness for them in this life. There are many examples of minor sins in all religions. Islam gives the example of talking excessively about matters which are not one's concern. In Judaism the example is given of being vain. An example of a Christian minor sin is telling a white lie. One could go on and on.

Things get much more interesting when it comes to the gravest sins as understood by those three faiths. The gravest sin in Islam is believing in multiple gods. The second one is murder. In Judaism the hierarchy is somewhat similar. Idolatry is understood to be the greatest sin. Murder is second. The same is true of Christianity, which puts faith in God at the top of the list, followed by murder and other divine laws which are enumerated in the Ten Commandments.

I suppose that a secular humanist would disagree with this hierarchy of grave, or mortal sins. He or she may argue that murder should be at the top of the list, since it can never be rectified, while believing or disbelieving is something that (a) cannot be judged by others, and (b) can change with time. I find this argument compelling, and I am not sure I can refute it.

Be that as it may, I am at once struck by the great similarity in the ordering of sin by the three faiths, and I find myself to be further confused the more I study the many theories about sin advanced by all three. That should not surprise us, because the same thing occurs in legal systems around the world, which are always redefining infractions, misdemeanors, felonies, and so on, and struggle with the question of finding the suitable punishment for each category.

What we do know for a fact is that man is expected to be able to tell right from wrong, and to strive to do that which is right. Anyone can make a mistake, but everyone is expected to correct it rather than repeat it. A sin becomes grave when it becomes a habit that cannot be shaken off, and which continues to color one's behavior to the point where one cannot tell right from wrong, as in the case for example of a habitual liar.

This is where prayer comes in. When you ask in your prayers forgiveness for your sins, you are expected to become aware of the wrong things you have done, and correct them. Otherwise, the prayer is meaningless.

To make matters more interesting, traditional Christian morality lists what is known as the "seven deadly sins" which threaten to destroy a person's moral fiber. Those are:

Wrath
Greed
Sloth
Pride
Lust
Envy
Gluttony

Here the term "sin" becomes even more confusing, since none of the above are specific sins one may commit, but rather personality traits that can lead to committing an actual, even a deadly sin. The Cambridge Dictionary defines them as "Those faults in a person's character that are thought to be the cause of all evil actions." Take, for example, lust. I recall President Jimmy Carter once telling his interviewer at *Playboy Magazine* that he sins because he lusts in his heart.*

Carter, a religious, "born again" Christian, was entering an interesting zone which is known in Judaism as "thoughts of sin." We are told in the Talmud that "thoughts of sin are worse than sin itself." How is that possible? Well, Jewish sages have offered many and diverse commentaries for this statement. The gist of those commentaries is that sin begins with a thought, and that thoughts of sin go unpunished and therefore leave a burden of guilt. Thus, the so-called "seven deadly sins" are the incubator where sins are hatched, and by controlling one's lust, anger, greed, and so on, one is less prone to sin.

Semantically, therefore, the term "seven deadly sins" is inaccurate. A more accurate term might be "seven human weaknesses that can result in a deadly sin." But then again, not being a Christian myself I would leave this issue to Christian scholars to resolve. As a religious evolutionist, I consider the great confusion caused by the concept of sin to be a major proof that all religions evolve, and those

---

*While many Jews found his statement somewhat odd, it was actually anchored in the New Testament where it says: "But I tell you that anyone who looks at a woman lustfully has already committed adultery with her in his heart" [Matthew 5:28].

religions which are frozen in time become a threat not only to themselves but also to others.

That said, human behavior always needs correcting. Praying for forgiveness for one's actions or just asking for forgiveness of others is an act of reconciliation, hence a positive action. In an otherwise unmemorable novel which ushered in the seventies in the United States called *Love Story* by Erich Segal, we find the statement "Love means never having to say you're sorry." Apparently, this one little statement made the novel a runaway best seller. Many, however, have since criticized and even ridiculed this statement, and John Lennon even offered an opposite version: "Love means having to say you're sorry every five minutes." The only way I can explain the surprising popularity of Segal's statement is that the seventies in the U.S. were a time of social upheaval and a search for new answers to life's questions, and this statement, which flies in the face of human experience, was a way of defying conventional thinking.

Historically, the three monotheistic faiths have put a great emphasis on the concept of sin in their liturgies. The key prayer of Islam, taken from the Quran's opening chapter (*Surah Al-Fatiha*), ends with a petition to God to guide us "not in the path... of those who wander astray," namely, the sinners. Christianity, and particularly Catholicism, has exceeded all three in espousing the concept of original sin and in putting great emphasis on penance. In Judaism, the Day of Atonement or Yom Kippur is one long recitation of sins which goes on from sunset on the eve of Yom Kippur to sunset the next day. During that twenty-four-hour period the word sin is mentioned hundreds of times.

One may wonder whether the liturgies of the three faiths have put excessive emphasis on the concept of sin. So much so that to many nominal followers of those faiths the word sin has become devaluated. In the chapter which discusses a new language of faith, I will attempt to answer this question.

18. SUFFERING

To understand prayer one must understand life. Prayer is both a reflection of and a reaction to life, or, if you will, a way of coping with life.

Life has been defined as an ongoing struggle which ends in death. When Macbeth hears about his wife's death he utters the famous words,

> *Tomorrow, and tomorrow, and tomorrow,*
> *Creeps in this petty pace from day to day,*
> *To the last syllable of recorded time;*
> *And all our yesterdays have lighted fools*
> *The way to dusty death. Out, out, brief candle!*
> *Life's but a walking shadow, a poor player*
> *That struts and frets his hour upon the stage*
> *And then is heard no more. It is a tale*
> *Told by an idiot, full of sound and fury*
> *Signifying nothing. (Macbeth, Act 5, Scene 5)*

Life, according to Macbeth, is "a poor player that struts and frets his hour upon the stage and then is heard no more." Now, if a monarch feels this way about life, what about the common man?

Job, the great sufferer of the Bible, cries out to God and says, "Man is born to suffer" (5:7). In fact, the Hebrew word used here is not "to suffer" but rather "to labor." We have seen earlier that the traditional Hebrew word for prayer is work or, more precisely, sacred work. We are taught that work ennobles, but also that work, or more so, labor, is, again to quote the Bard, "toil and trouble." When a woman is about to give birth, producing a new life, she "goes into labor" which, I am told, is very painful.

The world's leading religion, namely, Christianity, has as its symbol the image of a human being nailed to a cross, dying a terrible death. Here we have one person whose suffering enables those who believe in him find meaning in their own suffering, indeed, find salvation. Here we have the concept of vicarious atonement, namely, the sins of all, past, present and future generations, are expiated vicariously because of the suffering of one person. The believing Christian prays to the suffering savior whose death epitomizes all of human suffering combined. Next to the idea of the one God, this may be the most powerful idea ever conceived by the human mind.

The narrative of Buddhism is based on the story of a young prince named Gautama Buddha who leaves his father's palace one day and discovers human suffering. Having been raised in his father's palace, he was deliberately sheltered from any contact with the misery of life in the countryside. When he finally ventures out, he discovers pain and suffering, illness, and old age, and even comes face to face with death when he sees a corpse. This experience changes his life. He becomes a wandering beggar, and he begins his search for the causes of suffering. Eventually, the movement which would become known as Buddhism begins to emerge, based on the Four Noble Truths, which state that life brings suffering, that suffering is part of living, that suffering can be ended, and that there is a path that leads to the end of suffering. These ideas sum up the key teachings of Buddhism, the ultimate goal of which is known as nirvana, a transcendent state in which there is neither suffering, desire, nor sense of self, and the subject is released from the effects of karma and the cycle of death and rebirth.

Older than the story of both Christianity and Buddhism, is the story of Judaism. While Christianity is two thousand years old, and Buddhism is six hundred years older than Christianity, Judaism dates back nearly four thousand years to the times of its first ancestor known as Abraham. The story of the Jewish people from the day God orders Abraham to sacrifice his only child, who is spared at the very last moment, to the time I was born in the twentieth century when six million Jews were systematically murdered in Europe for no good reason, has been a story of suffering, persecution, and martyrdom. How the Jews have survived through all this is a great mystery. The Talmud was aware of this mystery centuries ago. According to Rabbi Yohanan, the people of Israel can be compared to the fruit of the olive tree, because oil can only be extracted from the olive by pounding and pressing, and so Israel returns to the right path only through suffering. Unlike Christianity and Buddhism, which have created orders of monks and nuns who live a life of poverty and abnegation, Judaism does not encourage the embracing of such ascetic practices. Jews do not choose to suffer, perhaps because they have had more than their fair share of suffering without looking for it. Be that as it may, all three faiths, as well as other faiths, are anchored in this universal reality. When one listens to the Jewish cantor chant the prayers, or to the Muslim muezzin intone his call to worship, or to the chanting of the mass, one hears the voice of human suffering.

People need to know that their suffering is not meaningless. Otherwise, life itself becomes meaningless. In fact, one could argue that the secret of a successful life is overcoming suffering in all its forms by turning adversity into victory. A life without hardship seldom results in any significant achievement. My third grade teacher in Israel always encouraged us to work harder by quoting the saying of the sages of Israel, "The reward is commensurate with the pain" (in Aramaic, *l'fum tzaara agra*). I guess an American teacher would say, "No pain no gain," which is essentially the same thing.

In a psalm attributed to King David, the praying king says, "God is close to the brokenhearted, and saves those whose spirit is beaten down." (34:18) This has always been the teaching of Judaism, and it became the teaching of Christianity and other religions as well. A faith that does not care for the poor and the suffering is no faith at all.

Inside the Statue of Liberty on Ellis Island in New York, we find the famous words of Emma Lazarus,

"Give me your tired, your poor,
Your huddled masses yearning to breathe free,
The wretched refuse of your teeming shore.
Send these, the homeless, tempest-tossed to me,
I lift my lamp beside the golden door!"

The United States is a nation of immigrants, many of whom escaped oppression and privations and were given the opportunity to work and study and make a better future for themselves and for their children. One group, namely, African Americans, were brought here for the most part by force or coercion and were made slaves. Those of us who are alive today are privileged to witness the enormous progress they have made toward equality.

19. REPENTANCE

Central to all religions is the belief in the individual's capacity to find redemption and make a fresh start. What is expected of the person who seeks redemption is to feel regret for wrongdoing, and to go through a process which each religion offers for inner cleansing and becoming mentally and spiritually prepared to make that fresh start.

To this day, some religions and sects within the major religions resort to extreme methods to accomplish this goal. One example is the custom of self-flagellation which, curiously, is found in both Shi'a Islam and in Catholicism. In neither case, however, this extreme practice of flogging oneself with chains or whips or even cutting oneself with knives is directly related to repentance, nor is it widely practiced.

In the case of Shi'a Muslims, it happen during a yearly ritual commemorating the martyrdom of Imam Hussein, whom the Shiites revere, and it is practiced in some Shiite communities in India, Pakistan, Iraq, Lebanon, and even in the United States and Australia. But it is frowned upon in Iran and prohibited in Saudi Arabia. Each year this ghastly event is reported in the world media and produces gory pictures of men and even boys lacerating themselves till their blood runs over their bodies and on the ground.

In Catholicism, self-flagellation is reminiscent of the flogging of Jesus prior to the crucifixion. For centuries, the practice of mortifying the flesh for religious purposes has been common in Christianity, especially in Catholic monasteries and convents. In the Middle Ages, a Roman Catholic sect known as Flagellants engaged in public flogging as a form of penance, but it was later excommunicated by the Church.

To this day, this practice can be found among Catholics in countries like the Philippines, Mexico, and Peru.

Prayer and repentance go hand in hand. In Judaism, one who goes into the house of prayer with impure thoughts or with a burden of guilt cannot pray effectively. The Talmud uses the example of someone who goes into the bath to cleanse his body while carrying on his back a bundle full of slimy creatures.

In Catholicism one can go at any time to the priest to confess a sin and ask for forgiveness. The penitent declares sorrow for sinning and the priest imparts absolution, saying:

God the Father of mercies
through the death and resurrection of his Son
has reconciled the world to himself
and sent the Holy Spirit among us
for the forgiveness of sins;
through the ministry of the Church
may God give you pardon and peace,
and I absolve you from your sins
in the name of the Father, and of the Son,
and of the Holy Spirit.

Typically, the penitent is told to recite certain prayers and give charity.

In both Judaism and Islam the concept of repentance is described as the physical act of turning away from evil and returning to God. Both religions emphasize the divine attribute of mercy. In Islam God is "the compassionate and merciful one," while in Judaism God is "a compassionate and forgiving God." The concept of the return to God is common among the Hebrew prophets. "Return, you mischievous children," (3:22) the prophet Jeremiah calls out to the Children of Israel, "and I will heal your mischievousness." Indeed, the return to God is the common theme of the Hebrew prophets.

God, according to both Judaism and Islam, loves the repenting or "returning" person more than the righteous person who does not sin. "Where the person who performs sincere repentance stands," the Talmud says, "a perfectly righteous person cannot stand." Indeed, there are very few perfectly righteous people at any given time. Most people are imperfect, and are error-prone. God is ever ready to forgive. All man has to do is feel remorse, admit his failing to do the right thing, and right the wrong.

In Judaism, the tenth day of the first month of the Jewish year is set aside for returning to God. It is called the Day of Atonement, or Yom Kippur. In the Book of Leviticus we are told: "For on this day atonement shall be made for you, to cleanse you, so that you may be cleansed from all your sins before your God." (16:30) The entire day is spent from sunset on the eve of the day to sunset at the end of the day in prayer, fasting, meditation, and soul searching, asking God for individual and communal forgiveness. At the end of that long day of fasting, one feels contrite, humble, and repentant by the effect of fasting and praying for hours on end while beating one's chest and repeating, "We have sinned, we have transgressed, we are guilty," and so on.

In Israel, where the majority of Jews are not in the habit of praying during the year, the entire country shuts down on Yom Kippur for twenty four hours. Cars are not allowed in the streets except for emergency vehicles, and an entire nation ceases its daily business and becomes part of a worldwide Jewish day of atoning for all personal and collective wrongs "from this Day of Atonement to the next Day of Atonement which will arrive for us for the good." To the Jew, during this twenty-four-hour period, God is available to forgive "all your sins and transgressions and wrongdoing," if you practice "prayer, and repentance, and charity."

The Day of Atonement, the Talmudic sages tell us, only atones after one has made amends to the person one has wronged. One must first "come clean" with the person one has wronged, and only then can forgiveness be granted. There are, however, wrongdoings for which the day cannot atone. One example is the case when one has caused others to sin, and there is no way to rectify what was done. Another example is murder, which can only be expiated upon death.

What is particularly striking about the liturgy of the Day of Atonement is the fact that the vast majority of the sins listed in the long recitations of sins which are repeated throughout the day have to do with the spoken word. Stealing, let alone committing murder, is not a common activity. But gossiping, cursing, lying, speaking in anger, and so on, are wrongs people commit on an ongoing basis. Here it is almost impossible to find a person who has not "sinned with the tongue." Even Moses, we are told, committed the sin of speaking in anger when he reprimanded the Israelites in the desert saying, "Do you expect me to draw water out of this rock?" for which he was punished by God who prevented him from entering the Promised Land. And even Jesus lost his temper and, to quote William Blake again, "gave with charity a stone." Speech is what makes us human. Speech is also what brings down the best and the brightest among us.

But the Day of Atonement is not the only time a Jew is expected to repent. Repentance is an ongoing process. One is expected to ask oneself every single day, have I wronged anyone? Have I failed to do the right thing? Introspection is the essence of our humanness. Striving to better ourselves as human beings is what prayer is all about. To pray mechanically and not mean what one says is not prayer. It is like telling someone "I love you" without meaning it. Prayer is "the service of the heart," not the mind. One must feel it to make it real.

20. THE AFTERLIFE

Man's greatest fear is death. It accompanies us from the moment we become self-conscious to our last breath. Upon waking up in the morning the believing Jew says:

I thank You, eternal and living King,
For in compassion You have restored my soul into my
body,
Great is your faithfulness.

A child's prayer popular in the Christian world for the past two hundred years says the following in one of its many versions:

Now I lay me down to sleep,
I pray the Lord my soul to keep,
If I should die before I wake,
I pray the Lord my soul to take. Amen.

Life, then, is a gift which is given to us every day of our life. But what happens when that gift is taken away from us? What happens when that day comes on which we no longer wake up?

Man has devised many theories over the centuries to answer this question. Central to these theories is the belief that the demise of the body is not the end of one's existence. Life continues after death in other ways. How specifically all of this happens is something for which every religion and every denomination and sect has provided its own answers. One thing, however, is quite clear: our life continues in the life of others, most immediately in the lives of the members of our family, but in a broader sense in the life of our community and our nation.

All of this, which is quite self-evident, is reflected in what we call communal prayer. When a family prays together, or when a faith community comes together in prayer, an affirmation of the continuity of human life beyond the life of the individual person takes place. The family or the community is joined together in a spiritual moment that transcends individual existence. It also ties together past and future generations, who have and will be joined together by the same prayer or ritual long before we were here and long after we are gone.

Another way of looking at communal prayer is a participation in a spiritual activity in which one turns away from one's temporal life and joins a higher life over which death has no dominion. Perhaps the best example of this is the prayer in both Judaism and Christianity derived from the vision of the prophet Isaiah in which the prophet goes to the Holy Temple in Jerusalem and witnesses the presence of God:

> *In the year King Uzziah died I saw God sitting on a throne, high and lifted up, and his train filled the temple.*
> *Above it stood the seraphim: each one had six wings; with two he covered his face, and with two he covered his feet, and with two he was hovering.*
> *And they all called one another and said, Holy, holy, holy, is the God of Hosts, the whole earth is full of His glory. (6:1-3)*

Holy, holy, holy. The Catholic Church calls this prayer the Sanctus. It is a key prayer in the Catholic mass. To Jews it is the *kedushah*, or Sanctification, which is the high point of the *amidah*, the central prayer of every Jewish worship service. The presumption in both faiths seems to be that these words, uttered by the angels or seraphim at the heavenly throne as they worship God, bring the human worshiper closer to God than perhaps any other prayer.

By uttering these words one is joining the heavenly hosts who are spiritual beings who live "in the presence of God" and are part of eternity. Thus, these words have the power to lift mortals above earthly existence and enable them to join the heavenly choirs. Indeed, the act of communal prayer is an imitation of an activity that transcends temporal life and reaches to the heavens.

All of this applies to the reality of the collective as a vehicle for transcending the limits of personal life. But it does not address the issue of personal existence beyond this life. Is there a life for each one of us after death? And if so, what is it?

It appears that two ideas dealing with these questions emerged in Judaism around the time of the birth of Christianity, namely, an afterlife and a resurrection of the dead. These ideas, which were espoused by Pharisaic Jews, were rejected by Sadducee Jews of the time. The Sadducees were the traditional Jews of their time, who followed the old law of the Torah literally. The Torah does not postulate either an afterlife or a resurrection of the dead. In the Hebrew Bible, one's afterlife is the children one brings into the world or other relatives who live after one is gone.

The Pharisees, on the other hand, were those who were formulating new laws and ideas extrapolated from the old Scriptures, which became the new Oral Law or Talmud. The intent here was to keep up with the changing times and revitalize the faith. This is how the afterlife and the resurrection came into vogue among Jews, and were also espoused by the new religion which centered around the person of Jesus of Nazareth, who himself died and was resurrected, and who brought the promise to his followers of life beyond the life of this world. Later, the new religion that sprung from that same source known as Islam will also embrace the belief in life after death and the belief in the resurrection of the dead in the time to come.

For centuries, both Judaism and Christianity have struggled with the questions of afterlife and resurrection, and still do. Both religions believe in the duality of a body and a soul as we saw in the Jewish and Christian morning prayers cited above. Man exists on two levels, corporeal and spiritual. The immortality of the soul seemed easier to grasp than the immortality of the body. It is easier to envision the soul departing from the body after death and going on to another life. A soul does not require food and does not have bodily functions. A living organism, on the other hand, existing in a new life, is very hard to imagine. So the belief in an afterlife became in most cases the life of the soul, not the body. As for the body, that was left in both Judaism and Christianity to a messianic time, an end of days, when a new earth will be created without the toil and trouble of this earth, and a physical resurrection would take place.

But even this was not so easy to accept. The great medieval philosopher of Judaism, Maimonides, had a hard time accepting physical resurrection. He struggled with it all his life, and as he was careful not to antagonize the Jewish scholars of his time, he tried to skirt the issue. He and his counterpart in Christianity, Thomas Aquinas, also sought to establish a hierarchy among those who achieve immortality, by limiting it to the ones who truly attain the knowledge of God, while others who do not attain it may not experience the afterlife, and, in the case of evildoers, those may be destroyed altogether.

Today, Jews differ in their belief regarding the afterlife and, even more so, the resurrection. To many it is an open question. To Orthodox Jews, it is a doctrine, as it is to Christian literalists. The official position of Reform Judaism is that the soul is immortal, but not the body.

There are many views on these matters to this day among different Christian movements. Jehovah's Witnesses, For example, deny the existence of hell. Instead, they hold that the souls of the wicked will be destroyed. The death that Adam brought into the world is spiritual as well as physical, and only those who gain entrance into the Kingdom of God will exist eternally. However, this division will not occur until Armageddon, when all people will be resurrected and given a chance to gain eternal life. In the meantime, the dead remain unconscious.

Seventh Day Adventists also believe that the dead are not conscious, and they liken death to sleep. The dead will not be "resurrected" until the second coming of Jesus Christ, or, in the case of the wicked, until after the millennium mentioned in the Book of Revelation. They do not believe in hell, but that evildoers will be judged and destroyed at the end of time.

Like the belief in God or in a messiah, the belief in life after the life of this world is purely a matter of faith, not of measurable data. The most concrete way of approaching it is to say that man in part of nature and that man's soul or spirit is part of a cosmic spirit we all share. This approach is shared by many faiths who posit that there is one God for all, and that all people are the children of the one God. The idea that each of our individual lives may be repeated in the future is something that Eastern religions and Western philosophers such as Nietzsche and Kierkegaard have put forth. In the final analysis, immortality takes on many different forms, and should not be dismissed out of hand.

Finally, a word about the belief in reincarnation.

Most people have heard of the Hindu or Buddhist belief in reincarnation. According to this belief, after one's death, the soul of the departed migrates, or transmigrates into another body. It can be a body of another person or an animal. Thus, one can be a banker in one life and a bug in another. When I first learned about this belief, probably in my early youth, I thought it was pure nonsense. I recall reading a story by Franz Kafka called "Metamorphosis," in which the protagonist, named Gregor Samsa, wakes up one morning and finds out he had become a cockroach. I thought Kafka had a wonderful sense of humor. But many years later, after I had grown older and wiser, I began to understand the logic of this belief. I finally understood why a humane belief system like Buddhism had made this idea its cornerstone.

What most people don't realize is that the idea of reincarnation reaches back to ancient Egypt, ancient Greece, ancient Israel, and to other cultures all around the world. Somehow, intuitively, many different people in many different ages and many different parts of the world have come upon it intuitively. In Hinduism, Jainism, and Buddhism, it became the centerpiece of those belief systems. In Judaism, for example, it became the domain of the Jewish mystics or Kabbalists. One could argue that in Christianity the resurrection and the second coming of Jesus are a form of reincarnation, and so on.

There is something very humane about the way the above-mentioned Eastern religions or belief systems have come to believe that a human soul can migrate into another form of life. What it says is that man must treat other creatures with respect and compassion. It also says that man must treat nature with respect and compassion, as we have come to learn of late in our new understanding of the great threat to our physical environment which we are all facing. So when all is said and done, those people in India centuries ago were not so misguided after all. Their beliefs, which once appeared so outlandish to the Western mind, have begun to make inroads in the West in our lifetime, and continue to do so. Perhaps the message they are sending us is that our birth and death are not the beginning or the end. Rather, they are way stations on the unending road of life, and that, in reality, we have been here before, and we will be here again.

21. THE EFFICACY OF PRAYER

There was a time when people put a great stock on prayer. At the dawn of time, according to the biblical narrative, the first two brothers, Cain and Abel, brought offerings to God. We read:

> *And it came to pass that Cain brought of the fruit of the ground an offering to God. And Abel also brought of the firstlings of his flock and of the fat thereof. And God turned to Abel and to his offering, but to Cain and to his offering He did not turn. And Cain was very angry, and he became morose. And God said to Cain: 'Why are you angry, and why have you become morose? If you do well, shall it not be lifted up, and if you do not well, sin lies at the door; and unto you is its desire, but you may rule over it.' And Cain spoke unto Abel his brother. And it came to pass, when they were in the field, that Cain rose up against Abel his brother, and slew him. (Gen 4:3-8)*

The presumption here seems to be that Abel was a righteous person, and so God accepted his offering, while Cain was sinful and therefore his offering was not accepted. And yet the text does not confirm this view, which has to be extrapolated from the next event, namely, Cain committing the first murder in history. Historically, offerings and sacrifices preceded prayer, and were intended to ingratiate oneself with the deity. But the general understanding has always been that one cannot bring an offering and continue to sin and expect to be forgiven. The same applies to prayer. As we have seen in the chapter on repentance, prayer is predicated on turning away from sin and being reconciled with God.

That said, however, there has always been an element of uncertainty in the process of prayer and reconciliation. There is no such thing as guaranteed prayer. If, for example, someone stole a goat and then returned it, and either made an offering for this sin or said the appropriate prayer, it does not follow automatically that forgiveness will be granted. God is not a heavenly accountant who keeps a ledger of sins with credits and debits. The math of heaven is much more complicated. One can only hope for God's favorable response, and continue to go about one's business hoping for the best.

Perhaps the most puzzling question of all time is why do good people suffer. In the story of Cain and Abel, the latter is taken to be a good person, and yet he dies at his brother's hands. Cain is assumed to be a bad person, but this is not confirmed. We are left with a puzzle, which will continue to haunt us every time someone whom we consider to be a good person suffers. And so the element of the unknown is always there in regard to life itself and in regard to prayer.

Organized religion expects its adherents to pray on a regular basis. But this does not mean that it guarantees anything in return. Religious teachers and preachers who assure their followers that saying a certain prayer will bring them good fortune are not being honest either with their followers or with themselves. The promise of good fortune is not something one can take to the bank, so to speak. If one wishes to be honest with oneself, then the definition of good fortune has to be very broad. "Who is rich," Jewish tradition asks, and it answers its own question: "He who is happy with his lot." Happiness does not depend on how much money a person has, but how one makes the most of what one has.

The ancient Greeks used to say that "The gods help those who help themselves." This saying became popular in the United States ("the gods" was replaced with "God,") which is a country founded on the principle of self-reliance. This principle was also followed by the people who raised me in what is now the State of Israel, so when I came across this saying in the U.S. for first time, it was easy for me to relate to it. Later, when I became a rabbi and finally a world traveler, it became increasingly clearer to me that people, so to speak, make their own good fortune. This did not make me give up prayer or faith in God. On the contrary, it made me realize that when I pray I should not entertain false expectations. God has given me brain and brawn so that I may use them. I look at it as a partnership. I am a partner in God's work of creation, and God is my partner who gives me far more than I can ever hope to give back. How can I give God anything closely resembling the sun, the rain, the earth, the ocean, and the ability to wake up each morning and greet the new day?

To me, prayer only makes sense within the context of this partnership. Again, going back to the earliest stories in the Book of Genesis, it is made clear from the outset that man is born with free will. Man is free to do right or wrong, and man has choices. Cain and Abel, the first two human beings to be born of a human mother, had a choice how to conduct themselves and what kind of offering they brought to God. This did not guarantee Abel a long life, nor did it mean that Cain's offering was going to be accepted. Cain, obviously, overreacted, and had to pay the price. Beyond that we seem to be left without answers. We have to accept the limitations of our human knowledge.

22. PRAYING FOR HEALING

While prayer may have its beginnings in the fear of the unknown, perhaps the most frequent reason for praying has been the search for healing and being restored to good health. In the Hebrew Bible, prophets like Elijah and Isaiah play the role of healers, and in the New Testament we have Jesus frequently healing the sick. In both instances, it is the plea to the Ultimate Healer, namely, God, which results in healing. Today, however, while members of Christian denominations such as Christian Scientists, Mormons, Pentacostals and others practice faith healing, Judaism leaves healing to the medical experts and uses prayer merely as a spiritual vehicle for enhancing the healing process.

Despite the unprecedented progress in all areas of medicine in our time, there is still a great deal medicine cannot treat or cure. The list ranges from certain forms of cancer to the common cold. Some medical experts have been arguing that all forms of cancer will never be completely eradicated. As for the common cold, unlike smallpox which has been relatively easy to eradicate, the common cold has many strains, and since it is not life-threatening, it has not been a priority in contemporary medical research.

The limitations of formal medicine have given rise to what is known as alternative medicine, which includes homeopathy, naturopathy, chiropractic, energy medicine, various forms of acupuncture, traditional Chinese medicine, Ayurvedic medicine from India, as well as holistic medicine. In addition, a new field of medicine is now being explored known as personalized medicine, which uses an individual's genetic profile to guide decisions made in regard to the prevention, diagnosis, and treatment of disease. The thinking behind personalized medicine is that no two patients are the same, and such things as a medical dosage cannot be applied equally to large groups of patients.

Since medicine does not have all the answers to health problems, it should not surprise us that the aforementioned forms of alternative medicine have been flourishing, and that spiritual healing which includes prayer continues to play such a prominent role in people's lives around the world, despite earlier predictions to the contrary by such widely influential thinkers as Karl Marx and Sigmund Freud. Marx called religion "the opiate of the masses," a way of keeping people obedient and oppressed and preventing the lower classes from bettering their lot.*

Freud also considered organized religion to be a negative force which he referred to as an illusion, and considered the repetitive nature of formal prayer to be a form of neurotic behavior. Writing in the early part of the twentieth century, the founder of psychoanalysis

---

*I recall a visit of Pope John Paul II to the Dominican Republic a few years ago, in which this popular and very humane pope celebrated a mass with some half a million people in attendance, during which he told the multitude consisting mostly of very poor people that they were fortunate to be poor, because they would be the first ones to go to heaven and enjoy eternal bliss.

believed that organized religion would soon wither away and disappear.

The long history of religion and medicine is both complicated and fascinating. Ancient civilizations in China, India, Babylonia, Egypt and later in Europe excelled in the development and practice of medicine, laying the foundations for today's medicine. At the same time, healing and religious faith went hand in hand in past centuries, as the natural and the supernatural were believed to be intertwined. It is only in the past two hundred years that religion and medicine have been going their separate ways. Nevertheless, the two continue to infringe on each other's domain, and the debate as to whether religion has helped or harmed human health continues unabated.

Much of what comes under the heading of medicine is what we call today folk or traditional medicine, which ranges from medicinal herbs to amulets. In my travels in Southeast Asia, in places like Singapore and Hong Kong, I have seen many stores selling medicinal herbs and home-made potions and ointments. In my childhood I recall seeing housewives using cupping, the attaching of glass cups with heated air to a sick person's naked back as a way to treat various illnesses. For centuries, this and other folk methods were used around the world. To this day, the vast majority of people in certain African and Asian countries rely on folk medicine.

Millions of people throughout time have believed in the healing power of prayer, and many still do. Among the branches of Christianity, Christian Science stands out as a movement which believes that the healing power of prayer is superior to human medicine. This branch of Christianity has been one of the more controversial religious movements in the United States, because some of its more zealous members would try to withhold medical treatment from a sick child, or would stop the use of a vital drug to prove the power of faith, with adverse consequences. Much of this has changed, but one thing that has not changed is the continued emphasis on prayer, particularly by religious movements inspired by Christian Science, such as the Unity Church which maintains a website where people are invited to participate in the ongoing experience of prayer.

Another Christian denomination that puts a great emphasis on health as one of the central concerns of religion is the Seventh Day Adventists. The Adventists follow a strict vegetarian diet, and are known for operating good hospitals throughout the U.S. and around the world. Interestingly, both the Christian Science and the Adventist movements were started by women, Mary Baker Eddy and Ellen G. White, respectively. I am not personally familiar with Christian Science, but I am quite familiar with Seventh Day Adventists, since my wife worked for several years as director of social services at one of their hospitals, the Washington Adventist Hospital in Takoma Park, Maryland, where this faith was first started. In some respects the Adventist religious practices are close to Jewish traditions, in that they espouse biblical dietary laws and the observance of Saturday rather than Sunday as the holy day of rest. But what strikes me the most about this branch of Christianity is their dedication to healing and the practice of medicine.

Medical studies have been conducted in the U.S. and elsewhere, using control groups and double blind, to find out whether prayer by a third party helps hospital patients with the healing process. Results have been mixed and inconclusive. It seems to me that those well-intended studies were missing the point. While I do believe in the healing power of prayer, I do not believe that praying for the healing for someone else can in and of itself cure that person. What I do believe is that there is a strong bond between body and mind, and perhaps body and soul. Much of illness is psychosomatic and often self-inflicted and self-prolonged. The human mind, which I consider to be a divine gift, has an amazing power over the human body. In my early years as rabbi on Long Island I conducted over one hundred Bar Mitzvah ceremonies every year (actually, over one thousand in seven years, which may be some kind of a record). Many of the grandparents of the Bar Mitzvah boys and girls were frail or in poor health, suffering in many cases from terminal illnesses. After two or three years of performing so many Bar Mitzvah services, I noticed that a large number of those grandparents died soon after that important family event involving their grandchildren. It became clear to me that in more than a few cases the grandparent would have died sooner, but the will to see the grandchild called to the Torah and to celebrate this event with the rest of the family kept the ailing grandparent going long enough to be able to participate in this milestone event.

My own medical history amply proves this point. The early years of my rabbinical career were quite stressful. This was due to several factors, some of which had to do with congregational life and some had to do with my own personal issues. Be that as it may, in my late twenties I was diagnosed with Crohn's disease, which more likely was bleeding colitis. I had repeated episodes till the age of thirty-six. In one instance I lost so much blood I had to be hospitalized and was given blood transfusions for a week, while I was being fed intravenously. Later on I was hospitalized again for hematuria, which was clearly stress-related. At that point my primary care physician, who was the son of a Christian minister, gave me some tips on doing meditation. He told me to concentrate on some insignificant item, clear up my mind, and only think about that item. I followed that exercise, and much of the stress I was under dissipated. Consequently, the hematuria disappeared. But what actually healed me from my intestinal ailment soon thereafter was a major career change. I was finally given the opportunity to take control of my own work, and those intestinal and digestive track ailments disappeared. It became clear to me that much of our illness is self-aggrevated. Another thing I learned to do over the years, before we were blessed with the flu vaccine, was to wish the common cold away. Every winter I would contract a cold, and every winter I told myself I could put mind over matter and I was able to get rid of the cold.

Can prayer heal? I believe that prayer, as a manifestation of the power of positive thinking, can heal. Having been exposed to meditation, I have also come to believe in the power of meditation, which comes to us from Eastern religions. The point of it all is quite simple. Our body, mind and spirit need to be able to operate in harmony, and we need to reach a good balance in our lives. Stress, being a mental excess, is the enemy inside of us. It throws our lives off balance, and it attacks our body at its weakest spot. In my case it was my digestive system. With others it can be the brain, the nervous system, the muscles, the joints, and so on. Restoring our faith in ourselves, and restoring our faith in the power of good in the world, is a powerful medicine.

23. PRAYING FOR PROSPERITY

Is it proper to pray for prosperity?

All religions agree that God or the gods reward good and punish evil. They further agree that faith and good works lead to a good life and to prosperity. But it is not common to find prayers in which a person actually asks God for property or riches. It came to me therefore as a surprise when I read a little book by a Christian teacher and writer named Bruce Wilkinson, who has had quite a large following in the U.S. and around the world, called *The Prayer of Jabez*. The book was first published in 2000, and has been widely read and seems to have affected many people's lives. The author quotes two verses from the last book of the Hebrew Bible, the Book of Chronicles, which reads as follows:

> *Jabez was more honorable than his brothers. His mother had named him Jabez, saying, "I gave birth to him in pain." Jabez cried out to the God of Israel, saying, "Oh that You would bless me indeed and enlarge my territory! Let Your hand be with me, and keep me from evil." And God granted his request.*
> *(I Chron 4:9-10)*

The Book of Chronicles contains long lists of genealogies of the Hebrew tribes, and does not, for the most part, make for inspiring reading. In the midst of all the genealogies and the chronologies we find the above two verses, which seem quite innocent. We have no idea who Jabez is, since this is the only place in the Bible where his name appears, and the passage is quite obscure and hard to translate. But we are told that he was honorable (actually, the Hebrew word means respectable or important), viz., a good person, and that he prayed ("cried out" means prayed) to God and asked for God's help and protection. So far everything is quite straightforward.

The one problem is that Jabez actually asks God for more land, presumably at the expense of his brothers and his tribe (the land was divided according to tribes and families). Wilkinson seizes upon the words "enlarge my territory" and proceeds to tell the reader that he had found out that reciting this prayer repeatedly has brought him great success, and that he highly recommends it to all his readers as a sure formula for gaining God's favor. He cites examples of people who had listened to his advice and kept reciting these words, and as a result became prosperous.

One cannot argue with faith. If indeed this formula worked for Wilkinson's followers, more power to them. But as I started to look deeper into the Jabez prayer phenomenon, I began to discover that among American evangelicals, particularly those who belong to large non-denominational churches, there is a strong movement that has been following what has been referred to as "prosperity theology." The pastors of those churches have been arguing in favor of prosperity, pointing out that material success has been demonized when, in reality, being prosperous gives one the opportunity to do more good by affording to be charitable. Hence prosperity is, religiously speaking, a good thing. One such pastor, T. D. Jakes, has viewed poverty as a hindrance to living a Christian life.

As can be expected, this concept has been criticized and denounced by some Christian leaders, who have pointed out that Christ himself stated in Mark 10:25 that "It is easier for a camel to go through the eye of a needle, than for a rich man to enter the kingdom of God."

One famous exponent of prosperity theology has been the Evangelical pastor Oral Roberts, who has argued that donations made to his church would have a "sevenfold" return from unspecified sources. On the other hand, an equally well-known Evangelical pastor, namely, Jerry Falwell, was highly critical of the movement, calling it heretical.

About one out of every four Americans belongs to Evangelical churches or movements within or outside of churches, which range from fundamentalists to non-conservatives and even progressives. Their beliefs vary widely, and cannot be generalized. But the idea of a so-called "prosperity theology" almost sounds to me like an oxymoron, since Christianity is founded of the idea that God loves the poor and the humble, an idea I as a Jew find quite appealing, since I espouse the words of the prophet Micah who said, "walk humbly with Adonai your God."

God, if you will, has been good to me and to my family, and while we are not multimillionaires, we are quite comfortable, and we live a good life and try to be as philanthropic as we can. I have never prayed to God to make me prosperous, and it has always been my impression that money in the hands of humans does more harm than good. Moreover, the sages of my faith teach us that the one who is truly rich is the one who is "satisfied with his lot." I have had contacts with many wealthy people over the years, including many powerful CEOs and famous entrepreneurs, and for the most part I have not found them to be happy because they were rich. There is a common belief among people who are not rich that if you gave them a large sum of money they would know exactly what to do with it, and they would be very happy. And yet, the story of those who "have won the lottery" is that quite often the unexpected bonanza brought them more grief than happiness.

In the Bible, God promises the Israelites who are wandering through the desert on their way to the Promised land that

> *If you keep in My statutes and My commandments,*
> *and do them; then I will give your rain in its season,*
> *and the land shall yield its produce, and the trees of the*
> *field shall yield their fruit. . . And I will turn to you, and*
> *make you fruitful, and multiply you; and will establish*
> *My covenant with you. And you shall eat old store long*
> *kept, and you shall take out the old to make room for*
> *the new. (Lev 26:3, 10)*

God does not promise the Israelites that each and every one of them will be rich if they keep the commandments. This is not even realistic. Everyone cannot be rich. The goal of an enlightened society is to eradicate poverty, not to make everyone rich. The idea here is that God will bless the land, and that everyone will have enough to eat and that society will be fruitful and will multiply, which is the greatest blessing in Judaism, far exceeding material wealth. Excessive wealth can be both a blessing and a curse. Americans who have amassed great fortunes, such as Bill Gates, Warren Buffet, and Mark Zuckerberg understand this all too well. All three have made the decision to give the lion's share of their wealth to help others, and are leaving a small portion of it to their children.

This is a proper use of wealth. Unfortunately, philanthropy is always practiced by a relatively small portion of the rich, which is why the Christian savior said long ago that "it is harder for the rich to get into heaven than for a camel to walk through the eye of a needle."

Praying for health and healing is perfectly legitimate. Praying for wealth is a symptom of an over-indulgent society and a trap set for the gullible by those who need to keep taxing their followers because they have gone overboard in building spectacular houses of worship and have become dependent on donors.

24. LIFECYCLE PRAYERS

From birth to death, there are moments in our journey through life that are sanctified. Those who reject religion and do not like the word sanctified, may react by muttering under their breath the word sanctimonious. And yet, even the most secular of mortals feels awe and wonder in the face of birth, rites of passage, the marriage ceremony, important anniversaries, death, and bereavement. Here is where life, culture, custom, tradition, personal and collective memory, hopes and aspirations merge and demand a proper human expression that is appropriate and dignified. If traditional or contemporary prayers and rituals are not present, then something else needs to take their place, such as poetry, music, personal testimonials, and so on. In his book *Psychoanalysis and Religion*, Erich Fromm argues that even secular communism in the Soviet Union was a form of religion, complete with parades and ceremonies and symbols and fiery speeches. A person, as part of organized society, needs a familiar format to frame important moments and set them apart from the ordinary daily routine which for the most part passes unnoticed and vanishes into oblivion. Historically, religion has provided this format, and for a large portion of the human race it still does.

People who do not regularly attend houses of prayer do become exposed to prayer at life cycle events such as birth, marriage, and funerals. On those occasions, prayer becomes personalized. The focus of the prayer ritual is the newly born, the bride and groom, or the deceased. The family and friends of the person on whose behalf prayer is offered, become personally involved in the ritual, whether or not they are in the habit of praying. Typically, such events are accompanied by meals, ranging from a light repast to an elaborate banquet. These are social functions that bring people together in either small or large numbers, and the food and drink become part of the ritual. Unlike a prayer service in a house of prayer, where the service is the main event, in lifecycle events the person is main event, while the prayers play a support role.

The main purpose of lifecycle rituals, however, is to bring the newly born, the young adolescent going through a rite of passage, the newlyweds, and the deceased into their faith or social community, where they share a common identity, common traditions, and common beliefs. When a Muslim baby is born, it is traditional to whisper in the baby's ear the key statement of the Muslim faith about the unity of Allah and the belief in Allah's messenger. When a Christian baby is baptized, the officiant at the baptismal font blesses the infant in the name of the Father and the Son and the Holy Spirit. When a Jewish baby boy is circumcised, he is welcomed into the covenant of Abraham, and given a Hebrew name. A baby girl is named and welcomed in the synagogue. In each case the newly born is inducted into the community of faith.

It is interesting to note that in Israel, where the majority of Jews are not religiously observant, new lifecycle rituals have been emerging, a clear indication that even without the traditional rituals, secular Israelis feel the need to affirm their bond with the historical Jewish community. Such new rituals include a *britah*, the feminine form of *brith*, or male circumcision, which in the case of the baby girl does not involve circumcision but rather baby naming, and bat mitzvah, the feminine form of bar mitzvah, in which secular text often replaces the traditional reading of the Torah.

In recent years, societies around the world have been undergoing profound social changes, which cut across national, cultural, and religious identities and redefine lifecycle prayer. In the Western world a growing number of Jews has been marrying non-Jews, which has given rise to a growing number of interfaith weddings. Such weddings often try to accommodate both religions, and necessitate a new kind of a wedding ritual. When such a couple starts having children, decisions have to be made whether the male child will undergo traditional Jewish circumcision, or whether the child will be baptized. It is commonly agreed by the parties that they have to choose one or the other.

In the case of a same sex marriage, be it Jewish or non-Jewish or an interfaith ceremony, the traditional words of either religion have to be modified. I recently attended a same-sex marriage of two Jewish men who are old friends of mine. The wedding for all purposes was a traditional Jewish wedding, but the vows had to be altered to fit the occasion. This couple has belonged for a long time to a gay Jewish congregation, where I attended services on more than one occasion and was impressed by the exuberance and camaraderie of the people in attendance.

Recently the new Pope, Francis I, speaking of gay priests, said, "Who am I to judge them?" While he did not change the Catholic Church's stand on homosexuality, he did take a giant step in acknowledging and rectifying prejudice against the LGBT community. The Catholic Church since Vatican II has been going through a sea change in regard to its practices and beliefs, and the process is far from over. While there has been progress as well as regression, the winds of change are blowing hard and more change is to be expected.

It appears that of the three religions, Islam is the one that is having the greatest difficulties keeping pace with the other two. But even in the Muslim world, which is torn by violence and terrorism, there are voices calling for change, especially among young people, and although what was recently known as the Arab Spring has turned into a winter, the story of Islam, like all major religions, is still being written, and change is bound to come.

Life is with people, and so is prayer. Nowhere is prayer more personal or more intimate than on lifecycle occasions. Such occasions have a spiritual dimension, and for lack of a better word, need to be sanctified. The word "sanctified" is derived from the root "to make holy." Something is holy when it is set apart from the profane, or the common run of everyday life. It has to be approached with dignity and respect. It is there to remind us that life is not a free for all but sacred. The birth of a child is a sacred moment, whether one is a believer or not. Marriage is not a casual event in a person's life. The word for marriage in Hebrew is *kiddushin*, which means "making holy." And the ritual of burial is where the deceased passes on from this life to the next world, where knowledge ends and a higher force takes over. When a Jew dies, the bereaved family recites the prayer known as Kaddish, which affirms the sanctity of God's name and of the gift of life.

In short, lifecycle events bring believer and nonbeliever alike face to face with the greater reality that each person is part of something greater than one's own self, something which demands articulation either in the form of a prayer or in some other dignified manner.

25. YEARLY CYCLE PRAYERS

People have a personal and a communal calendar which fills every year of their lives with important dates on which they celebrate key events in their own lives as well as important events in the life of their country and their faith. Like the lifecycle events discussed in the previous chapter, here too people face what we may call prayerful events. Here prayer or a special song or a hymn or an appropriate address is in order.

In his famous song I Just Called to Say I Love You, the popular American singer and songwriter Stevie Wonder refers to several American holidays on which you call someone you love, and makes the point that he is calling on "just another ordinary day" to say "I love you," as if to say, "I don't need an excuse to call you and tell you that I love you." However, the flipside of this heartfelt statement is the need to say certain things on those holidays which befit the occasion, starting with "Happy New Year" and ending with "Merry Christmas." Indeed, the American year starts with this first greeting and reaches its high point with the second.

On the Catholic calendar the first day of the year is dedicated to Mary, Mother of God, and each day thereafter is dedicated to a specific saint. When I lived Guatemala, a very Catholic country, there seemed to be a daily event dedicated to the saint of the day. Earlier, when I lived in Uruguay, a nominally Catholic country which separated church from state early on, this close attention given to saints was absent from daily life. Uruguayans do not pray nearly as much as Guatemalans. It seems to me that these two countries in Latin America represent two extremes. In the United

States, on the other hand, religious pluralism and religious freedom have resulted in more respect for religion, more so than in other parts of the Christian world, and more tolerant attitudes within most religions and in their dealings with other religions. To me, this is a model for other societies to emulate.

But no matter what country one lives in, there is a universal need to celebrate the important dates in one's personal and communal calendars. My youngest child just celebrated her birthday, and I was overwhelmed by the outpouring of love and photos on Facebook from family, friends, and acquaintances. I say to myself, my wife and I brought this little baby into the world, and now, not so many years later, she is having such an impact on the lives of so many people. In my tradition, the birth of a child is something that happens among three partners: mother, father and God. So all I can say is: Thank you, God.

Each religion has its history, which is celebrated in its yearly holidays or holy days. While Christianity and Buddhism and even Islam are transnational religions, Judaism is rooted in the national narrative, land, and language of the Jewish people. The Buddha, Jesus, and Mohammed do not belong to one nation. Judaism, however, is the faith and culture of one people with one history. While the first half of Jewish history was spent in the ancestral land of the Jews, the second half was spent around the world. But no matter where Jews have been living, they continue to pray for the return to their ancestral land, they continue to celebrate the agricultural festivals of that ancient land, namely, Sukkot (Tabernacles), Pesach (Passover), and Shavuot (Pentecost), and they continue to read their Holy Books in the original

Hebrew, as if they are still living in the Land of Israel.

Perhaps the most beloved Jewish holiday is Passover. In my years as rabbi on cruise ships I celebrated Jewish holidays at sea. The one holiday that attracted the most people has been Passover. Even non-Jews asked to be included in the festive meal of the holiday, during which a special prayer book known as *Haggadah* is used to follow elaborate rituals involving traditional symbolic food, and even includes a game of hiding a piece of matzo, or unleavened bread, which has to be found by the children in the group so that the long celebration can be concluded. Passover has many layers of meaning, but its central message is the liberation of the Hebrew slaves from Egyptian bondage, an event dating back 3300 hundred years which still resonates not only with Jews but with all freedom-loving people everywhere.

The most solemn event on the Christian calendar is Easter, which celebrates the resurrection of Jesus Christ from the dead. Easter is linked to Passover since the whole chain of events leading up to the crucifixion and the resurrection begins with the story of Jesus and his disciples celebrating the feast of Passover, an event which later becomes known as the Last Supper. Here again the universal impact of a holiday celebrated by a small nation in a small corner of the Middle East becomes evident. I have witnessed the celebration of Easter in different parts of the world, and I wonder whether any other religious celebration of any other religion equals it in scope.

Another Jewish holiday that has a universal meaning is Hanukkah, which celebrates the victory of the small Hebrew nation led by Judah Maccabee against the vast army of the Syrian-Greek king Antiochus who sought to replace the

Hebrew faith in God with the idols of Greece. Both Passover and Hanukkah resonate with both religious and secular Jews. The believers see the "hand of God" in the miraculous liberation of the Hebrew slaves from Egyptian bondage and the victory of the Maccabees over the Greeks, while the non-believers celebrate the heroism of the ancient Hebrews who on two occasions, one thousand years apart, won a victory over world powers.

A Christian holiday that has both a religious and a secular meaning, particularly in the United States, is Christmas, which celebrates the birth of Jesus Christ. I have witnessed the deep spiritual meaning of Christmas by attending Christmas Eve services, including midnight mass, once in a convent as a guest of a young nun whom I befriended while serving as a young rabbi in Cleveland, Ohio. The chanting of *Silent Night* has stayed with me all these years, and one does not have to be a Christian to appreciate the depth of faith this simple Christmas carol invokes. On the other hand, as was explained to me by several Christian clergy, Christmas for many people in America has become a purely social and even commercial event, in which the original message of the festival has all but disappeared.

Both Christmas and Hanukkah and, more recently in America, an African American festival called Kwanzaa*, as well as similar festivals around the world, must have had

*Started in the sixties as an African American protest against White America, and as a substitute for Christmas, but now celebrated by many African Americans along with Christmas.

their origins in pre-monotheistic times as winter holidays, when the days grew shorter and night came early with the first frost and snow, and fire was used to chase away the darkness and the cold. Thus, Hanukkah is known as the Festival of Lights, in which candles are lit each night for eight nights, while Christmas has given the English language the expression, "all lit up like a Christmas tree." All human holidays have their roots in antiquity, and all are interrelated in many ways.

But apart from all the festivals and celebrations of the year, the Jewish faith has given its people and the world the most important one of all, which is the Sabbath. Both Christians and Muslims have their own Sabbath, observed on Sunday and Friday respectively. The Sabbath in the Jewish faith is of such importance that it was included in the Ten Commandments as the fourth commandment, bridging the first three which deal with God and the remaining six which deal with human conduct. The commandment reads:

> *Remember the Sabbath day and keeping it holy. Six days you shall labor and do all your work, but the seventh day is a Sabbath to Adonai your God. On it you shall not do any work, neither you, nor your son or daughter, nor your male or female servant, nor your animals, nor any foreigner residing in your towns. For in six days Adonai made the heavens and the earth, the sea, and all that is in them, but he rested on the seventh day. Therefore Adonai blessed the Sabbath day and made it holy. (Ex. 20:8-11)*

One could argue from a purely secular point of view that

here we have one of the earliest pieces of social legislation in human history. In antiquity, slaves worked seven days a week and never had a day off unless they were sick. When the Roman occupiers of the Land of Israel found out that the Judean faith mandated one day a week of doing no work, they concluded that those Judeans were lazy people. They also called them atheists, because they did not have visible gods. Clearly, the Sabbath was a revolutionary idea, much ahead of its time.

As I mentioned at the beginning of the book, I was not raised in an observant family. But I recall as a child of eight I used to wake up on Saturday morning, my day off from school, and I would sing,

This day is honored above all other days
For on this day the Rock of Ages rested.

This is a traditional, twelfth century song, which was not popular among us in the forties and fifties in Israel, but which I must have picked up somewhere. I wasn't only singing because I was happy to be off from school. I actually believed that the Sabbath was a gift from God, even though my teacher who was a fervent socialist Zionist rejected this idea.

As I grew older and hopefully wiser, I came to appreciate the Sabbath more and more. The great Jewish thinker, Abraham Joshua Heschel, called the Sabbath "an island in time." Indeed, it is an invisible island a Jew is allowed to go to once a week, where the life of the spirit takes over, leaving the life of work and worries behind for twenty four hours, Allowing one to refresh body and soul through prayer and song and festive meals, and by focusing on the people rather than the problems of one's life.

I imagine that for the devout Muslim and for the devout Christian the feeling is similar. I have seen Muslims at prayer on their Sabbath, and I felt the depth of their piety and serenity. I have attended church services on Sunday and felt something similar. But I still feel that for me the Jewish Sabbath is indeed "the queen of days," that it is, as described by the Jewish sage Leo Baeck, "a taste of the world to come." Nature repeats its seasons every year, and it is from nature than humans have borrowed their yearly cycle of celebrating life and giving thanks. But humans have also discovered a force in nature which, according to the Jewish prayer book, "changes the seasons and arranges the stars in heaven according to His will." No matter what name we give to this invisible force in nature, and no matter in what language we address this force, it is this articulation which, to use a phrase from the old Reform Jewish prayer book, "endows our fleeting days with abiding worth."

Each person has a personal history and also a collective history. During each year, we celebrate both our personal and our collective histories. We celebrate family events, and we also celebrate the events of our culture and tradition. Prayer enables us to do both. It is a way of putting our feelings into words which are not casual or tentative, but which have been sanctified by time and usage, and have become words of prayer. Above all else, prayer is a celebration of time. In the Jewish tradition we have a prayer called the *shehecheyanu*, or "who has kept us alive." It says:

Blessed are you, Adonai, king of the universe,
Who has kept us alive, and has preserved us,
And has enabled us to reach this time.

Ultimately, prayer is a celebration of life.

26. THE SABBATH AS A DAY OF PRAYER

In Judaism, the Sabbath, which starts on Friday night and ends on Saturday night, is the day when one is expected to leave the work day world and dwell in the spiritual world of repose. It is the day when prayer takes on a special meaning, for on that day the heart takes over, not the body or the mind.

Christians and Muslims have their own version of the Sabbath, but it is not as completely separated from the rest of the week and sanctified as the Jewish Sabbath. As was mentioned, the commandment to sanctify the Sabbath day and keep it holy appears in the Ten Commandments, which makes it one of the cornerstones of Judaism. Few things in Judaism are more important than keeping the Sabbath and making it holy. Traditional Jewish life revolved around the Sabbath, which is the day of prayer par excellence, the day on which the Jews are at one with their soul and with their Maker.

The Sabbath is where the idea of a weekend originated. In antiquity, there was no such thing as a day of rest. The ancient Romans considered the Jews lazy because they refused to work for one day each week. The Romans, of course, had their slaves who worked for them seven days a week, while they, the masters, could rest whenever they felt like it. For the working person, the weekend is something one looks forward to. For the Jew, the seventh day until recent times has been the weekend. When I grew up in early Israel, our weekend was only one day. In recent years, Friday was added to the weekend, to make it a two-day weekend as is the custom in the West.

The Hebrew thinker Ahad Ha'am commented that "More

than the Jews kept the Sabbath, the Sabbath kept the Jews."
There is much truth to this statement. The masses of Jews
in Eastern Europe were mostly poor and had to work hard
to eke out a living. But on the Sabbath the Jew felt like a
prince. He called the Sabbath the Queen of Days, and he
saw himself as the son of the queen. He would sing, "*Avinu
malkenu*, our Father our King, we have no king but you." He
would recall the words of the great sage Akivah: "Happy are
you O Israel, for who purifies you, and before whom are you
purified? Before your Heavenly Father." (Talmud Yoma 86a)

During the Sabbath, which lasts from sundown to
sundown, the Jew is not allowed to be angry or sad, lest he
detract from the holiness of the day. It is the day dedicated to
the Most High, and one cannot come before the Most High
with a tense or a long face. No matter what else happens in
one's life, the Sabbath is a timeout from one's troubles. One
of the most compelling stories in Jewish lore that illustrates
this truth is the following:

> *The story is told about Rabbi Meir who was teaching*
> *at the House of Study on the Sabbath in the afternoon,*
> *when his two sons died.*
> *What did their mother do? She put them in bed and*
> *spread a sheet over them.*
> *When the Sabbath ended Rabbi Meir came home and*
> *said to her,*
> *Where are my two sons?*
> *She told him, they went to the House of Study.*
> *He said, I waited for them at the House of Study and I*
> *didn't see them.*
> *She gave him the glass of wine for the Havdalah prayer*

*and he said the prayer. He repeated his question:
Where are my two sons?*

*She said, they went somewhere and they are coming
back. She gave him food and he ate.*

*After he said the blessing she told him: I have a
question for you.*

He said, ask.

*She said, my master, a man came and left something
with me for safekeeping. Now he came back to claim it.
Should I have given it back to him"*

*He said, my daughter, if someone is keeping
something, should he not return it to its owner?*

*She said, If not for what you say, I would not have
returned it.*

*What did she do? She took him by the hand and led
him up to the room at brought him close to the bed,
and took off the sheet. He saw the two dead bodies
lying on the bed.*

*He started crying, my sons, my sons, my teachers,
my teachers, my sons in the ways of the world but my
teachers because you clarified for me the words of the
Torah.*

*At that moment she said to him, Rabbi, did I not tell
you we have to return what was loaned to us to the
rightful master?*

*Yes, he said, God gave and God took away. May God's
name be blessed.*

*Said Rabbi Hanina: She was able to console him with
those words, and he calmed down. Regarding this it
was written: "A woman of valor who can find."(Midrash
Mishle 31)*

The Jew has always felt that on the Sabbath he lived in another dimension, best described as "sacred time." One of the meanings of the word sacred is separate from everything else around it. That sacred time cannot be violated. One must make every effort not to trespass or violate it, which is what Rabbi Meir's wife, whose name was Bruriah, and who was considered a scholar, did. How many women were or are capable of doing such a thing? The time of prayer is a sacred time, but the time of the Sabbath prayer is the most sacred of all.

The main lesson of the sanctity of the Sabbath seems to be that prayer as communion with God is not a casual or voluntary activity. It is at the heart and core of faith. Just as the body cannot survive without food, the soul cannot survive without prayer. A life without prayer is a life detached from one's soul and from the soul of the world. It is a life, to paraphrase Heschel's expression, without awe and wonder. Every person is confronted with the mystery of life and death, and every person needs to feel that life is more than just a biological phenomenon without meaning or purpose in a cold and empty universe. Bruriah's behavior did not diminish her as a mother. Aware of the higher purpose of life, she knew how to sanctify life by not letting death have the upper hand over life. To her, as an informed Jew, the Sabbath represented the eternity of the soul. Yes, her two sons were taken away from her, but this was not the end. The Sabbath had to be celebrated, life went on. In the words of the New Testament which were reworked into a great poem by Dylan Thomas:

And death shall have no dominion.
Dead men naked they shall be one
With the man in the wind and the west moon;
When their bones are picked clean
And the clean bones gone,
They shall have stars at elbow and foot;
Though they go mad they shall be sane,
Though they sink through the sea
They shall rise again;
Though lovers be lost love shall not;
And death shall have no dominion.

In his book *The Essence of Judaism*, Rabbi Leo Baeck refers to the Sabbath as "a taste of the world to come." The world to come is the Jewish concept of the afterlife. This long life which is to follow our much shorter life is seen by the major religions as a place of repose, meditation, and uninterrupted bliss. Many times on a peaceful Sabbath one feels a stirring of another, better life. The same is true about other faiths. Mark Twain in his novel *Huckleberry Finn* captures some of that feeling in his own humorous way in the following paragraph:

When I got there it was all still and Sunday-like, and
hot and sunshiny; the hands was gone to the fields;
and there was the kind of faint dronings of bugs and
flies in the air that makes it seem so lonesome and like
everybody's dead and gone; and if a breeze fans along
and quivers the leaves it makes you feel mournful,
because you feel like it's spirits whispering—spirits
that's been dead ever so many years—and you always

think they're talking about you. As a general thing it
makes a body wish he was dead, too, and done with it
all.

While Twain appears to be more profane than reverent, behind the humor he captures the feelings of a boy who is lonely but who feels the presence of spirits from the past on a "Sunday-like" day, and seems to wish he could join them and be done with his own nomadic life down the Mississippi which is quite precarious. Somehow, in a roundabout way, Twain connects with the otherworldliness of the Christian Sabbath, as I have always connected since my own childhood with the otherworldliness of the Jewish Sabbath.

27. PEACE OF MIND

No matter how deeply we become involved, cognitively or spiritually, in the actual meaning or the spirit of the prayer, prayer per se seems to have the power to change our state of mind from anxiety and preoccupation to a state which is either one of partial or full calm, or what is generally referred to as peace of mind. The very act of opening a prayer book and sitting down or standing up to pray in a house of prayer seems to have a calming effect on people. What I find particularly striking is the state of deep calm of those who practice meditation in the Asian religions. They seem to take leave of the troubles of life and enter another state of being, one of deep communion with one's soul or with a cosmic soul to which one entrusts one's life. While there are different levels of prayer, by joining others in prayer one feels instinctively that one has entered a special space and a moment in time where negative feelings and bad thoughts are suspended and inner peace prevails.

But prayer in and of itself cannot provide lasting peace of mind. If the praying person has some personal issues or something that troubles his or her mind, prayer all by itself will not suffice.

It is interesting to note that almost any dramatic work in world culture depicts human conflicts, in which the protagonists are troubled and have no peace of mind. A good example is the scene in *Hamlet* in which the young prince is about to avenge his father's death after Hamlet's father was murdered by his brother, Claudius, who is now the new king. When Hamlet finds Claudius, the king is deep in prayer. It occurs to Hamlet that if he kills Claudius while the new king is praying, he will end the king's life at the moment when the king was seeking forgiveness for his sins, sending Claudius's soul to heaven.

It seems that young Hamlet was wrong thinking that by praying alone the new king could have had his crime forgiven. Even Claudius knows that simply by praying the murder will not go away and he will not be forgiven. Claudius says,

> But, O, what form of prayer can serve my turn?
> 'Forgive me my foul murder'?
> That cannot be; since I am still possess'd
> Of those effects for which I did the murder,
> My crown, mine own ambition and my queen. (III:iii)

The author knows that there is no forgiveness for Claudius until he begins to show remorse by starting with giving up the crown, his ambition, and his marriage to Hamlet's mother. In other words, as we have seen earlier in the discussion of prayer and repentance, prayer by itself cannot ensure forgiveness or enduring peace of mind. The crime committed by Hamlet's uncle preys on the new king's mind, and it also affects everyone around him. No one in this dark play, perhaps Shakespeare's greatest, enjoys peace of mind. Not the king, not Hamlet, not Ophelia, no one.

I have recently seen a Russian movie called *Leviathan*. It tells the story of the harsh life of people living in present-day Russia in a remote town in the north, run by a corrupt mayor and corrupt officials, who are supported by a corrupt Russian Orthodox priest. Here religion and prayer are presented in a negative light, as part of the complete corruption of the town. The only remedy the town's people have for this sorry state of affairs is the endless consumption of vodka, which keeps many of them in a constant state of inebriation.

What *Hamlet* and *Leviathan* have in common is the validation of the old cynical comment that sometimes "religion is the last refuge of the scoundrel." Neither Claudius nor the corrupt mayor and his willing collaborators achieve peace of mind by praying. What we learn here is that prayer and rituals per se are not sufficient for achieving enduring peace of mind. A guilty conscience will haunt a person no matter how much praying that person does.

What these two dramas, which are separated by about five hundred years (actually more, since the original story of Hamlet dates back some four hundred years before the time of Shakespeare), seem to convey is that peace of mind is by no means an easy thing to achieve, let alone define, since no one lives in isolation from others and is able to order one's life with disregard to external events and other people. The corrupt mayor and the corrupt priest in the Russian movie are not at peace with themselves, and the entire town suffers as a result.

It reminds me of a story dating back to ancient Greece, about a stoic philosopher who always taught his students not to show strong emotions of any kind, but instead to react calmly to whatever happened to them. One day this philosopher was teaching his class when a messenger came from the battlefield and told him that his son had just died in battle. The old stoic started crying and beating his chest, as his students looked on in amazement. When he finally calmed down, one of them asked him, master, you have taught us not to show strong emotions, and now that you have suffered this great loss you contradict yourself. Yes, the old man replied. You are right. I shouldn't have reacted like this. But I couldn't help myself.

The long-term purpose of prayer is to bring about a *lasting change* in the way we deal with our life. Earlier in the book I referred to prayer as a pep talk we give ourselves. This is a short-term solution. What people are really looking for when they pray is to achieve a state of mind in which they have sufficient mental and emotional fortitude to face what Shakespeare called "the slings and arrows of outrageous fortune" and prevail. It is what the author of the Psalms meant when he said,

Adonai is my light and my salvation—
whom shall I fear?
Adonai is the stronghold of my life—
of whom shall I be afraid?
(27:1)

Many times over the years when I found myself in a state of great uncertainty and anxiety I would turn to the Book of Psalms and read passages like this one. As I grew older many of the Psalms became engraved in my mind, and I am now able to recite them from memory. It is small wonder that both the Jewish and the Christian faiths are so dependent on the Book of Psalms for finding faith and fortitude.

It may be easy to preach peace of mind, which all religions do, and which psychologists do as well. But in reality, more often than not, it remains an elusive goal. Lao Tzu, the Chinese founder of Taoism, said, "Life is a series of natural and spontaneous changes. Don't resist them–that only creates sorrow. Let reality be reality. Let things flow naturally forward in whatever way they like." This saying (which in the West is usually expressed as "go with the flow") seems to create a critical divide between East and West, which may have a direct bearing on the issue of achieving peace of mind. What we have here is a dichotomy of Eastern and Western thinking.

I am not sure where Islam fits in this dichotomy, so for the purposes of this discussion I would argue that Christian civilization, in which I would include post-Holocaust Judaism as well, is militant and proactive, while Eastern civilization, primarily Hinduism and Buddhism in all of their varieties, are, for the most part, passive and acquiescent. It is no accident that Mahatma Gandhi, the father of present-day India, was able to defeat the British Empire and force it to leave India through nonviolent civil disobedience. Gandhi, who espoused both Hinduism and Buddhism, was deeply aware of the nonviolent nature of those religions. As for Christianity, he said famously, "I like your Christ, but I do not like your Christians. Your Christians are so unlike your Christ."

It is small wonder that, in the West today, Buddhism, at least as a social philosophy, has been making considerable inroads. To this day, Christian civilization and, since the birth of the state of Israel, Jewish civilization as well have been entangled in ongoing wars. Without analyzing the reasons for this or taking sides, suffice it to say that cultures which are militant and proactive are prone to produce more restlessness and tension than cultures which tend to be nonmilitant and passive. For this reason, it appears that Buddhists, for example, enjoy more peace of mind than Christians. I think back to the time in my life which I mentioned earlier, when my physician, the son of a Protestant minister, prescribed meditation when I suffered from an intestinal ailment due to great stress at work, and how well it worked for me. Here Eastern religions have a great deal to teach us Westerners who are goal-oriented, ambitious, and highly competitive.

Peace of mind is arguably life's greatest gift. What good is wealth or power or fame without peace of mind? The rich man who cannot sleep at night because he is worried what the stock market may do the next day is not a happy man. The leader who is troubled because he is afraid of assassination is not a happy man. And the famous movie star who takes drugs to cope with his or her stressful life is certainly not a happy person.

When we reconsider what has been discussed thus far in this book, it becomes clear that peace of mind has everything to do with what we have considered so far. We have started with the question why people pray. We have seen that people need to reach out beyond themselves to be able to face life's trials and tribulations and attain that inner peace that enables them to cope with that which lies beyond their control. Early on we discussed what is known as the Serenity Prayer, which asks for serenity to accept the things we cannot change, the courage to change the things we can, and the wisdom to know the difference. What this prayer makes clear is that the things we cannot change are the ones that deprive us of our peace of mind, not the things that we can change, or the ability to tell the difference. Over time we learn how to change the things we can change and tell the difference. But the things we cannot change, most critically the loss of a loved one, put us to the test of recovering our inner peace and going on living.

Moreover, the reason why prayer as an integral part of living is not a sometime thing but rather an ongoing activity is that peace of mind needs to be reinforced continually. Here I am referring to prayer in its broadest sense. Not only attending the house of prayer or opening the prayer book every day and praying privately, but also putting oneself in a mode of prayer or meditation, of being aware of one's ongoing relationship with a higher force, and reminding oneself that no matter what we are never alone.

To me as a Jew, the traditional Jewish prescription for peace of mind still holds. It consists of three words enunciated during the Jewish High Holy Days: *teshuvah, tefilah, tzedakah*—reconciling oneself with one's Maker; engaging in prayer; and performing good deeds. This is a religious definition, but it can also be expressed in secular terms. The end goal of both is the same: to be a good person. A good person can achieve peace of mind more readily than one whose hands or heart are not clean. Taoism may preach passivity, and Judaism may preach proactiveness. But either way inner peace can be achieved provided one follows the words of the Book of Psalms,

> *Who shall ascend the mountain of the Most High*
> *And who shall dwell in the holy place?*
> *He who has clean hands and a pure heart,*
> *Who has not taken My name in vain*
> *And has not sworn deceitfully. (24:34-4)*

* * *

Here are some examples of peace of mind prayers in various religions:

Christian

*Almighty God, We bless you for our lives, we give you
praise for your abundant mercy and grace we receive.
We thank you for your faithfulness even though we are
not that faithful to you. Lord Jesus, we ask you to give
us all around peace in our mind, body, soul and spirit.
We want you to heal and remove everything that is
causing stress, grief, and sorrow in our lives.
Please guide our path through life and make our
enemies be at peace with us. Let your peace reign
in our family, at our place of work, businesses and
everything we lay our hands on.
Let your angels of peace go ahead of us when we go out
and stay by our side when we return. In Jesus' name,
Amen.*

Muslim

*Inner peace is the source of all peace. When a person is
at harmony with himself, he is able to live in harmony
with others.
Allah says: "When you enter houses, greet yourselves
with peace." [Qur'an, 24:61]
Believers recite the following words in all of their
prayers: "Peace be upon us and upon Allah's pious
servants."*

Hindu

OM. May our organs, speech, Prana, eyes and ears be nourished.
May all our senses become strong.
Upanishad says all that the World is Brahman.
We don't reject Brahman, may Brahma not reject me.
Let there be no rejection, let there be no rejection at all in us,
let us concentrate on ourselves, all those ways of righteous living told in Upanishads be in us! Be in us,
OM Peace, Peace and Peace.

Jewish

It is written: "God is my refuge and my strength, a very present help in time of trouble" (Psalm 46:1).
Help us to feel that help. Let Your presence be a light within to dispel the darkness. Let Your nearness, Your silent speech within the heart, be a comfort to us. We pray for the courage to carry on in the face of disappointment, for the wisdom to learn from adversity, for the strength to build a new and better life. Your spirit can transform affliction into salvation; enlighten us, therefore, that we may look to the dawn of a new day with confidence and trust. May hope abide beyond the moment's loss. For You, O God of hope, are our sustaining power, even when we have fallen. Keep us from self-recrimination. Give us peace of mind and contentment of spirit. Amen.

Sikh

*You are the Ocean of Water, and I am Your fish. Your
Name is the drop of water, and I am a thirsty rainbird.
You are my hope, and You are my thirst. My mind
is absorbed in You. Just as the baby is satisfied by
drinking milk, and the poor person is pleased by seeing
wealth, and the thirsty person is refreshed by drinking
cool water, so is this mind drenched with delight in the
Lord. Just as the darkness is lit up by the lamp, and
the hopes of the wife are fulfilled by thinking about her
husband, and people are filled with bliss upon meeting
their beloved, so is my mind imbued with the Lord's
Love. The Saints have set me upon the Lord's Path. By
the Grace of the Holy Saint, I have been attuned to the
Lord. The Lord is mine, and I am the slave of the Lord.
O Nanak, the Guru has blessed me with the True Word
of the Shabad. - Guru Arjan.*

Jain

*Peace and Universal Love is the essence of the Gospel
preached by all the Enlightened Ones. The Lord has
preached that equanimity is the Dharma. I forgive
all creatures, and may all creatures forgive me. Unto
all have I amity, and unto none, enmity. Know that
violence is the root cause of all miseries in the world.
Violence in fact is the knot of bondage. "Do not injure
any living being." This is the eternal, perennial, and
unalterable way of spiritual life. A weapon, however
powerful it may be, can always be superseded by*

a superior one; but no weapon can be superior to
nonviolence and love.

Baha'i

Be generous in prosperity, and thankful in adversity.
Be fair in thy judgment, and guarded in thy speech.
Be a lamp unto those who walk in darkness, and a
home to the stranger.
Be eyes to the blind, and a guiding light unto the feet of
the erring.
Be a breath of life to the body of humankind, a dew to
the soil of the human heart,
and a fruit upon the tree of humility.

Native American

O Great Spirit of our Ancestors, I raise my pipe to you.
To your messengers the four winds,
and to Mother Earth who provides for your children.
Give us the wisdom to teach our children to love, to
respect,
and to be kind to each other so that they may grow
with peace in mind.
Let us learn to share all the good things you provide
for us on this Earth.

Sufi

O Almighty Sun, whose light clears away all clouds,
We take refuge in you. Guide of all people, God of all

deities, Lord of all angels,
We pray you to dispel the mists of illusion from the
hearts of the nations,
And lift their lives by your all-sufficient power,
Your ever shining light, your everlasting life,
Your heavenly joy and your perfect peace.

Tibetan Buddhist

May you be at peace,
May your heart remain open.
May you awaken to the light of your own true nature.
May you be healed,
May you be a source of healing for all beings.

28. WAR

In the 1980s, Argentina, which was ruled at that time by a military junta, decided it was time to take possession of the British Falkland Islands, which are located out in the South Atlantic on the way to Antarctica. Having spent a day in the Falklands during the height of summer, I had to wear a heavy coat and gloves because of the cold wind and the persistent rain that greeted us upon landing and kept us company until it was time to leave. I wonder whether too many Argentinians would have chosen to settle in that harsh place which is favored by penguins.

After Her Majesty's troops won the war for the Falkland Islands, the Archbishop of Canterbury, Robert Runcie, who was appointed by the then-prime minister, Margaret Thatcher, said a prayer for the dead on both sides of the conflict, which did not please the "Iron Lady." The Archbishop was breaking with the time-honored tradition of memorializing the troops in the name of the Christian Savior as they fought against another Christian nation who, quite obviously, was in the wrong. Somehow, "forgiving your enemy" was being disregarded by the victorious prime minister.

For centuries, Christian nations have fought each other in the name of the same Savior. Clergy on either side of the conflict would offer prayers on behalf of their country's troops and ask the Savior to grant victory against "the enemy," since theirs was always the just cause. In World War One, rabbis in France would ask God to bless the French troops, while rabbis in Germany would ask the same God to bless the German troops. How exactly this heavenly calculus worked is hard to tell. God must have had a very hard time trying to decide whose prayers should be heeded.

The idea of God as a "Man of War" goes back to the Hebrew Bible, where God "fights" on the side of the Israelites. When the Hebrew slaves are liberated from Egypt, God performs the great miracle of the splitting of the Red Sea, letting the fleeing slaves go across on dry land. When Pharaoh's chariots arrive and gallop through the opening in the sea, the water on both sides rises and closes over them and they all drown. After this miraculous rescue, Moses and all Israel sing a song of victory and say, "Adonai is a man of war whose name is God" (Exodus 15:3).

The idea of God as a Man of War is common to all ancient cultures. The Greeks and the Romans had a god in charge of war to whom they turned when seeking victory against their enemies. In fact, all the ancient gods were gods of war. There were very few years of peace in human history, and it was a given that all nations fight each other, with each believing that god is on their side and will come to their rescue. When a certain nation was defeated and lost its sovereignty, its god was defeated as well, and lost its legitimacy.

The Archbishop of Canterbury understood the absurdity of asking the Christian Savior to help Britain defeat another nation who believed in the same savior. The battle to retain control of the Falkland Islands was a political issue, not a spiritual one, and prayer was not the appropriate vehicle for its execution. Enlightened nations no longer fight wars in the name of God, or at least are not supposed to. Yet because the scriptures of one's faith are held sacred for all time, those ancient beliefs which people have followed for centuries are still with us today. One can only hope that they are with us metaphorically and not as articles of faith.

Here again, as in the case of referring to God as father and king, we learn that as human thought and values change over time, so does our understanding of God, and therefore the way we pray. Prayer that does not take cognizance of human progress keeps us chained to antiquated concepts and values, and fails to deal with reality as we know it today. This problem exists today in all religions and all social philosophies. It is felt keenly among Catholics around the world, in particular in the United States, who question many of the stands of their church's hierarchy, and it is a huge problem in the Muslim world, given the fact that essential human issues, such as the rights of women, are yet to be addressed by many of the scholars and leaders of Islam. The praying world continues to be divided between those who pray as though we are still living in the Middle Ages, and those who look for ways to reconcile the text of the prayers with the text of today's reality.

It is hard for me to believe that God was ever a "Man of War." My understanding of God is of a cosmic moral principle that abhors war and all other forms of human conflict. "Where is Abel your brother?" God says to Cain after Cain kills his brother. He then says to him, "The blood of your brother is crying to me from the earth." In rabbinical Jewish lore there is a legend about the Israelites celebrating the demise of the Egyptian soldiers in the Red Sea, during which time Moses refers to God as a "Man of War." The rabbis tell us that God says to the Israelites, "My children are drowning in the sea," "and you are celebrating?" Those rabbis two thousand years ago understood that God was not a man of war, but rather a compassionate God who cares about all his creatures and abhors war. Clearly, here Moses receives an indirect rebuke from the rabbis, who were pacifists and whose values were centuries ahead of their time.

In the twentieth century the world was torn apart by two world wars and other localized conflicts that changed the human condition forever. Not only were more millions of military personnel and civilians killed by human action than in any other century in history, but also human values such as progress and the ennobling influence of culture and art became bankrupt. We are yet to recover from this blight as we move deeper into the twenty-first century. In the chapter about prayer and the Holocaust we will take a closer look at this problem.

One term that has been used by all major religions and is still heard today in some parts of the world is the term "holy war." In my opinion, this is clearly an oxymoron. War is anything but holy. While defensive war is sometime necessary to stop deliberate aggression, and while self-defense is rightly considered necessary at times, it is always a necessary evil. Here again the language of prayer is found wanting. Prayer books everywhere speak of "us" and "them," with "us" always being the righteous ones, and "them" the evil ones, and of victory over the "enemy." Once again, as I am sure the archbishop of Canterbury would agree with me, those prayer books need to be revised. One paragraph which I have penned for this purpose is the following:

Dear God, may we first exhaust every possible avenue available to us to resolve this conflict peacefully before we go to war. And if we must wage war, may we be able to inflict as little damage as possible in life and limb as

we enter this conflict. May there be as few mothers and
fathers as possible on both sides of the conflict who
will have to grieve over lost life.

I for one do not believe that religion per se is the cause
of wars. Rather, religion is often used as a convenient excuse
to wage war, and as a crutch to justify what is otherwise
an immoral act. In the words of Bob Dylan's popular song
Blowin' in the Wind, "How many years will it take till he
knows that too many people have died?" Too many people
have died since the day I was born in 1939, six months before
the outbreak of the worst war of all time, and the world has
yet to learn the lesson that we are courting our own doom.
Praying for victory in war should be a thing of the past if we
stand a chance to make it to the next century.

29. WORLD PEACE

The fondest wish of the great majority of the human race is peace, and yet as of this writing there are violent conflicts all around the globe. Is it because while most people pray for peace, there are those in and out of power who only want peace on their own terms, and therefore resort to violent action to have their way?

Since the end of World War Two, the United States has been playing the role of peacemaker around the world. One of the notable accomplishments of these American efforts has been the peace agreement in Northern Ireland that was brokered mainly because of the mediation of U.S. Senator George Mitchell in 1995. The violent conflict in Northern Ireland raged for three decades with no end in sight. Those of us who lived through it did not think it would ever end.

Mitchell, the son of an Irish father and a Lebanese mother, was well suited for the role of peacemaker. I heard him speak a few years later at the University of Maryland, at which time he had been sent by President Barack Obama to the Middle East to make peace between Israelis and Palestinians. Mitchell told the audience that one thing he had learned from the bitter conflict in Ireland was that no mother wants her child to die, and therefore there is always a good basis on which to build a peace agreement.

What Mitchell did not take into account was that Palestinian organizations like Hamas were able to convince Palestinian mothers that if their children became suicide bombers and died for the cause of Palestine, they would become martyrs who, according to the faith of Islam, would achieve a glorious life in heaven, and would defeat their enemy. Unfortunately, Mitchell was not able to replicate in the Middle East what he had accomplished in Ireland.

In all of recorded history there has hardly ever been a year without people fighting a war somewhere. Today we are living through what seems to be a clash of civilizations. As the world has become more mobile than ever before in history, and as people travel across continents and the world is becoming multinational and multicultural, people around the world are engulfed in violent conflicts with no end in sight.

Much of it has to do with the problems of the Arab world. For the most part, Arab nations have not been successful in becoming competitive members in today's highly technological and scientific world community. An attempt was made in the recent popular upheaval known as the "Arab Spring" to free this vast portion of the human race from the shackles of poverty and oppression. But the euphoria that started in Tahrir Square in Cairo, Egypt, in 2011, which resulted in the resignation of Egypt's President Hosni Mubarak, only lasted about a year. Instead of gathering momentum and spreading throughout the Arab world, the tidal wave that started at that square and seemed so full of hope, led to an inept regime that replaced Mubarak, and, as many have observed, "spring" turned into "winter."

Once again, as had happened ten years earlier with the events of 9/11, perpetrated by Islamist terrorists, new mutations of al-Qaeda and the Taliban have been rearing their ugly heads in the Middle East and in Africa, and once again the world community is being subjected to horrific events such as the mass murder of school children in Pakistan, the decapitating of foreign journalists in Syria, the use of children as human shields by the Hamas in Gaza, and the kidnappings of Christian girls by Muslim terrorists in Nigeria.

In view of all this, does world peace have a prayer?

The answer I hear from most people whom I ask this question is no. No, it is hopeless. Man is doomed to live a life of perpetual conflict, with no relief in sight.

And yet, I choose to be an optimist. My optimism stems from my knowledge of the history of my people. The people of Israel, a numerically small people yet a giant of the human spirit, have defied the laws of history for the past 3300 years. By all logic, they should have long disappeared from the face of the earth. But the logic of the Jewish spirit defies common logic. Evil empires come and go, but the Jews are still here. Jews have a mission in this world. The mission is to repair the world in the image of the kingship of God. "The earth is God's and the fullness thereof," we read in the Book of Psalms (24:1). The emissaries of evil seek to appropriate the earth, but they always fail, because it is not theirs to appropriate. War and conflict is not the will of the people. It is the will of those who are against the people, and only care about themselves.

Is it worth praying for world peace? I believe it is. Even if it won't happen in our lifetime, I choose to believe it will happen eventually. "Your kingdom come," and "He will establish His kingdom," are the words pronounced by the Lord's Prayer and by the Kaddish. This is the greatest yearning of the human race. By keeping this yearning alive we ensure that someday, at long last, it will happen.

Here are some prayers for peace from several belief systems:

Baha'i Prayer for Peace

O God! Establish the great peace.
Join, O God, all hearts together.
Kind Father, God! Gladden our hearts through
the fragrance of Your love. Brighten our eyes through
the Light of Your guidance. Delight our ears with the
melody of Your word, and shelter us in the
Stronghold of Your providence.
You are mighty and powerful, You are forgiving.
You are the One who overlooks the shortcomings of all
humankind.

Buddhist Prayer for Peace

May all beings everywhere plagued
with sufferings of body and mind
quickly be freed from their illnesses.
May those frightened cease to be afraid,
and may those bound be free.
May the powerless find power,
and may people think of befriending
one another.
May those who find themselves in trackless,
fearful wilderness—the children, the aged,
the unprotected—be guarded by beneficial celestials,
and may they swiftly attain Buddhahood.

Hindu Prayer for Peace

> *Oh God, lead us from the*
> *unreal to the Real.*
> *Oh God, lead us from darkness to light.*
> *Oh God, lead us from death to immortality.*
> *Shanti, Shanti, Shanti unto all.*
> *Oh Lord God almighty, may there be peace in*
> *celestial regions.*
> *May there be peace on Earth.*
> *May the waters be appeasing.*
> *May herbs be wholesome, and may trees and*
> *plants bring peace to all. May all beneficient*
> *beings bring peace to us.*
> *May thy Vedic Law propagate peace all*
> *through the world.*
> *May all things be a source of peace to us.*
> *And may thy peace itself, bestow peace on all*
> *and may that peace come to me also.*

Jain Prayer for peace

> *Peace and Universal Love is the essence*
> *of the Gospel preached by all*
> *Enlightened Ones.*
> *The Lord has preached that equanimity*
> *is the dharma*
> *Forgive do I creatures all,*
> *and let all creatures forgive me.*
> *Unto all have I amity, and unto none enmity.*

Know that violence is the root cause of
all miseries in the world.
Violence, in fact, is the knot of bondage.
"Do not injure any living being."
This is the eternal, perennial, and unalterable
way of spiritual life.

Muslim Prayer for Peace

In the name of Allah,
the beneficent, the merciful.
Praise be to the Lord of the
Universe who has created us and
made us into tribes and nations
That we may know each other, not that
we may despise each other.
If the enemy incline towards peace, do
thou also incline towards peace, and
trust God, for the Lord is the one that
hears and knows all things.
And the servants of God,
Most gracious are those who walk on
the Earth in humility, and when we
address them, we say, Peace.

Native American Prayer for Peace

Oh Great Spirit of our
Ancestors, I raise
my pipe to you.
To your messengers the four winds, and

to Mother Earth who provides
for your children.
Give us the wisdom to teach our children
to love, to respect, and to be kind
to each other so that they may grow
with peace of mind
Let us learn to share all good things that
you provide for us on this Earth.

Shinto Prayer for Peace

Although the people living
across the ocean
surrounding us, I believe
are all our brothers and sisters,
why are there constant troubles in
this world?
Why do winds and waves rise in the
oceans surrounding us?
I only earnestly wish that the wind will
soon puff away all the clouds which are
hanging over the tops of mountains.

Zoroastrian Prayer for Peace

We pray to God to eradicate all the
misery in the world:
that understanding triumph
over ignorance,
that generosity triumph over indifference,
that trust triumph over contempt, and

that truth triumph over falsehood.

Sikh Prayer for Peace

*God judges us according
to our deeds,
not the coat that we wear:
that Truth is above everything,
but higher still is truthful living.
Know that we attain God when we love,
and only victory
endures in consequences of which no
one is defeated.*

Christian Prayer for Peace

*Blessed are the peacemakers,
for they shall be known as
the Children of God.
But I say to you that hear, love your enemies,
do good to those who hate you,
bless those who curse you
pray for those who abuse you.
To those that strike you on the cheek,
offer the other one also,
and from those who take away your cloak,
do not withhold your coat as well.
Give to everyone who begs from you,
and of those who take away your goods,
do not ask for them again.
And as you wish that others would do to you,*

do so to them.

Jewish Prayer for Peace

May we see the day when war and bloodshed cease
when a great peace will embrace the whole world
Then nation shall not threaten nation
and humankind will not again know war.
For all who live on earth shall realize
we have not come into being to hate or destroy
We have come into being
to praise, to labor and to love.
Compassionate God, bless all the leaders of all nations
with the power of compassion.
Fulfill the promise conveyed in Scripture:
"I will bring peace to the land,
and you shall lie down and no one shall terrify you.
I will rid the land of vicious beasts
and it shall not be ravaged by war."
Let love and justice flow like a mighty stream.
Let peace fill the earth as the waters fill the sea.
And let us say: Amen.

30. PRAYER AFTER THE HOLOCAUST

As of this writing, seventy years have passed since the greatest crime in all of human history was committed. I am referring to the systematic murder of millions of innocent Jewish men, women and children. Genocides have been committed all throughout human history. But this time it was different. Typically, a genocide is a spasm of collective violence caused by an actual motive, be it economic, territorial, ideological, and so on. When the German or Germanic people under the leadership of a gang of criminals known as National Socialists, or Nazis for short, undertook the task of ridding the world of all the people of Jewish faith, culture, and ethnicity, there was no logical reason for it, other than the fact that in a highly anti-Semitic Europe Jews were an easy scapegoat. Instead, there was a total rejection of all the teachings of the great secular and religious thinkers of the human race throughout the ages. The law of "might is right" took over, and humanity lost its moral compass.

Hitler predicted that the world would eventually forget this event, as it forgot the genocide committed by the Turks against the Armenians (or earlier by the Germans against the Herero tribe in Namibia), and so on. He was wrong. True, the world has a short memory, but this time the world is not able to forget. This time the moral fiber of the world was broken and it still hasn't healed.

The beautiful prayers about love and peace in the previous chapter today sound hollow. In light of the events of the first two decades of the twenty-first century many people no longer believe that universal peace is possible. Man, the argument goes, is doomed to live in perpetual conflict and may even put an end to life on this planet as we know it. Pessimism is no longer the domain of the few. It is widespread. Indeed, it has become palpable. I find myself these days surrounded by it, and I know of no easy answers.

And yet, I know three things. First, I know that this is not the first time pessimism and even despair have gripped human society. The saying, "the world is going to the dogs," has been heard throughout history. You can find it the ancient Egyptian inscriptions and ancient Greek writings, and you can find it in the stories of creation in the Hebrew Bible. And yet, all those civilizations have left a lasting mark on the human race which continues to inform us today. Second, during my own lifetime I have lived through wars and famine and despair, but I have also enjoyed many of life's blessings and I have lived the good life. Third, as a man of faith I believe that where there is life there is hope.

What is prayer? Prayer is saying yes to life. It is an expression of the human spirit that refuses to let evil take over; that refuses to give in to despair; that refuses to stop believing better days are ahead. I cannot blame those who have given in to pessimism. After Auschwitz, it is a miracle there are still those, like myself, who believe in God. But then again, the present-day heirs of Hitlerism in the Middle East and in Europe and elsewhere who murder the innocent and spread fear around the world expect all people of good will to give up, so that they can take over. This indeed would be tragic, and must not be allowed. Even if we may feel that prayer has become meaningless, we must find a way to pray, to hope, and to believe that good will always win in the end.

In the chapter which discusses the need for a new language of prayer, we will show how the event known as the Holocaust has rendered many of the words of traditional prayer obsolete, and how the great religions can begin to articulate new words or give new meanings to some old words that will be in keeping with the new reality under which we live today.

This is by no means an easy thing to do. But some of this process has already begun in Christianity, in Judaism and in other religions around the world. Much more needs to be done, and as time goes on one can only hope that all enlightened faiths will be able to bring life and belief closer together. In short, one can relegate Auschwitz to the dustbin of history, but to use the words of Scriptures, when God became aware of the first human murder and said to Cain, "The voice of your brother's blood is crying out to Me from the earth," Cain could not run and he could not hide. Crime has consequences, and the crime of the Holocaust has consequences for generations to come.

When Germany was losing the war, Hitler said that Germany had no right to go on living if she lost. A delusional leader, he did not believe in the power of prayer or in the good in man. To him man was a predator, and the more ruthless man was the better chance he had to prevail. Hitlerism is not dead. It is rearing once again its monstrous head around the globe, and it must be stopped. Evil is real, it is not just the absence of good, as some thinkers would have us believe. It has a life of its own, and that perverse life is the enemy of humanity. To ignore evil is to invite disaster. One major function of prayer, both communal and personal, is to pray for good to prevail.

The Western world, from Berlin to Paris to New York to Buenos Aires, is dotted with memorials to the Holocaust.

Each year more memorials—ranging from commemorative plaques to sculptures to museums—are being added. The Jewish people in particular and the world in general have taken to heart the command never to forget. It is my belief that the Holocaust will never be forgotten. It was not just six million Jews who were senselessly murdered. Human conscience itself became a casualty of human evil. Can man pray without a conscience? Not likely. Restoring human conscience is the main task of prayer in our time.

One could also look at the history of our time and see how language has been so debased in the past one hundred years that it has prompted some great scholars like George Steiner and great writers like George Orwell to suggest that human language has become altogether bankrupt, and can no longer be trusted.

One good example of this outlook is the book *1984* by George Orwell. Orwell, writing in 1949 after World War Two and the Holocaust, and at the beginning of the Cold War between the Soviet Union and the West, describes an imaginary totalitarian state run by Big Brother (one of several terms invented by Orwell which have become part of the language), in which the life of the individual person has become completely controlled by the state and subjected to secret surveillance and propaganda. People are constantly brainwashed with such slogans as "war is peace" and "hate is love" and so on. Human language is completely devaluated, and human life becomes a dreary affair which is hardly worth preserving.

One of the greatest language scholars of our time, George Steiner, has written extensively about the devaluation of language in the twentieth century. In an interview about the devaluation of human language caused by Hitler and by Nazi Germany, Steiner says,

> He [Hitler] is one of the greatest masters of the language. As are [Martin] Luther's pamphlets asking that all Jews be burned. German language has—all languages can have it—but in the German language, Hitler drew on a kind of rhetorical power which, in a way that is perhaps peculiar to German, allies highly abstract concepts with political, physical violence in a most unusual way. . . And [Hitler] was easily a genius at that, absolutely no doubt about it. (See Ron Rosenbaum, Explaining Hitler)

Tyrants like Hitler and Stalin and Mao sought to eradicate religion and replace it with anti-person political systems, but they have all failed. Their lofty words and slogans have proven to be hollow and detached from reality. The human race refused to let go of its traditional beliefs. Prayer has not disappeared as a human way of using words to reach out beyond the here and now. The power of the words of the world's liturgies continues to inspire and energize a weary humanity that has undergone unimaginable ordeals and still does. It appears that the power of the words of books like the Hebrew Book of Psalms will always be with us. Some texts are irreplaceable. They are for the ages. They will be around as long as there is human life on this planet.

31. THE DETRACTORS OF PRAYER

In his book *God Is Not Great: How Religion Poisons Everything*, the late English author and leading atheist Christopher Hitchens has the following to say about prayer:

> *There is no need for us to gather every day, or even every seven days, or on any high and auspicious day, to proclaim our rectitude or to grovel and wallow in our unworthiness. We atheists do not require any priests, or any hierarchy above them, to police our doctrine. Sacrifices and ceremonies are abhorrent to us, as are relics and the worship of any images or objects. (p. 6)*

His fellow atheist, Richard Dawkins, in his book *The God Delusion*, has the following to say about God:

> *The God of the Old Testament is arguably the most unpleasant character in all fiction; jealous and proud of it; a petty, unjust, unforgiving, control-freak; a vindictive, bloodthirsty, ethnic cleanser; a misogynistic, megalomaniacal, sadomasochistic, capriciously malevolent bully. (p. 31)*

These two Englishmen, Dawkins and Hitchens, represent what has been referred to as the "New Atheism," the name given to a group of science-oriented writers, which also includes the Americans Sam Harris and Daniel Dennett. Harris wrote a book called *The End of Faith*, which advocates an end to religious faith as the evil force it is, and its replacement by a secular benevolent ethic. The commercial success of these authors indicates that people who call themselves atheists or are interested in the atheistic point of view are not few, either in the U.S. or the UK, perhaps more so in the UK. But what is interesting and not so easy to explain is that the two countries, which are so culturally close to each other, differ greatly in their approach to religion and science. The United States, which was not established as a religious society but instead introduced a separation of church and state, is to this day a very religious country, while the United Kingdom, which has always had a state religion, has become a vastly secular society. According to a Pew Research Center study dated May 1, 2014, 55 percent of Americans pray every day. Another study suggests that church attendance in the U.S. stands at 39 percent, while in the UK it is only 12 percent. In fact, it appears to be less than 2 percent, if we do not count England's growing Muslim population. Ironically, the strongest Jewish group in the UK is the Orthodox, which is the most ritualistic branch of Judaism, while in the U.S. it is the non-Orthodox, which is more liberal and tolerant, represented mainly by the Reform and the Conservative movements.

The problem with the afore-cited books is that they look to have it both ways. On the one hand, they take the ancient scriptures out of context and judge them against today's reality. On the other hand, they discuss them in their ancient context and fail to see any difference between them and the pagan world in which they were composed. In other words, both the old and the new testaments were composed in a world that practiced slavery, gave women few rights, and was steeped in superstitions and magic. And yet both contain social laws that are centuries ahead of their time, and both seek to replace superstitions and magic with a belief in a higher force that remains central to the lives of most people on this planet to this day. The scriptures are the record of our history both before and after this spiritual transformation. What is most significant about those scriptures, particularly the Hebrew Bible, is that it is a brutally honest book. It does not seek to embellish or sugarcoat the lives of Abraham or Moses or David. It shows them as erring human beings who are far from being saints, any more than people like Hitchens or Dawkins are saints. This, somehow, got lost on those authors.

One of the most revered personalities in the UK is the cosmologist Stephen Hawking, whose recent book is called *The Grand Design*. The book is described on Amazon as follows:

> *According to quantum theory, the cosmos does not have just a single existence or history. The authors [Stephen Hawking's and Leonard Mlodinow] explain that we ourselves are the product of quantum fluctuations in the early universe, and show how quantum theory predicts the "multiverse"—the idea that ours is just one of many universes that appeared spontaneously out of nothing, each with different laws of nature. They conclude with a riveting assessment of M-theory, an explanation of the laws governing our universe that is currently the only viable candidate for a "theory of everything": the unified theory that Einstein was looking for, which, if confirmed, would represent the ultimate triumph of human reason.*

One review of the book by a major American weekly gleefully announced that this book may indeed provide proof at long last that God does not exist.

The urge to do away with God and get rid of such ostensibly antiquated and irrelevant practices as prayer seems to flourish in both countries, and certainly in many other countries as well. I have always felt that religion is routinely blamed for the ills of the world, mainly because Christianity has had a history of intolerance and abuse of power, while Islam today is known to most people as a religion of terrorists and suicide bombers. As for the other religions, they too have their share of bigotry, prejudices, superstitions, and bad behavior.

The problem with this outlook is that none of the major religions teaches bigotry or intolerance. Those who persecute and kill people in the name of their religion violate the teachings of their own faith. This is what people like Hitchens and Dawkins fail to understand or choose to ignore. A careful reading of their books shows that they take the text of the scriptures of both Judaism and Christianity out of context and make what appears to be a strong case for the two testaments as being primitive and barbaric, because Moses and Jesus knew nothing about quantum physics and space travel, which makes us today so superior to them.

This is what I would call the common mistake of the scientist or the scientifically-minded person. A cosmologist is by these authors' definition superior to a theologian. According to Dawkins, theology is a farce, because it does not pass the test of science. What Dawkins and his colleagues fail to grasp is that, to quote Pascal again, "The heart has its reasons of which reason knows not." The task of faith is not scientific investigation. This, at least since the Enlightenment and especially among open-minded theists, is left to the scientist. Faith is concerned with human behavior, with justice and fairness and the sanctity of life (the word sanctity is anathema to people like Dawkins). Hence the scientific knowledge we possess today has nothing to do with Moses or Jesus. Dawkins chooses to vilify the God of Moses and Jesus, and Hitchens chose to live a prayerless life. This is their prerogative. But their cavalier attitude is not worthy of men who respect, nay, revere, science, and it makes one wonder whether the bigotry they impute to religion is not their own bigotry.

Personally, I find it demeaning to dignify those two with a lengthy rebuttal. They need to lower the volume of their rhetoric by a few decibels (in the case of Hitchens it's too late). Instead, I would rather take this opportunity to say that science is far from being close to solving the mysteries of the universe, let alone giving humanity the emotional solace it sorely needs in the face of all the evil in today's world. I respect the right of anyone to call herself (or himself) an atheist, as more than a few of my friends and close relatives do. But at the same time that I do not claim to know for a fact that God indeed exists (*a ciencia cierta*, as we say in Spanish), it is clear to me that no one can prove that God does not exist. Here the proof is not mathematical. It uses other criteria to which the scientist does not have access.

Personally, I prefer the agnostic to either the absolute believer or the absolute atheist. Both the absolute believer and the absolute atheist claim to know more than they actually know. Neither can prove the existence or non-existence of God. But the agnostic is the one who makes the honest statement that he or she can neither prove nor disprove the existence of an ultimate authority in the universe. This, of all the other possibilities, seems to me to be the most honest approach.

Let us for a moment assume that God, as Dawkins would have it, is indeed an illusion. In Spanish we say, *de ilusiones se vive* (one lives on illusions). For someone in love, the loved one is the most wonderful person in the world, although objectively speaking this may not be the case. For a mother, her child can do no wrong, although every child can do wrong. For a patriot, his or her country is the best in the world, although this is usually not true. But is it wrong to feel love, or maternal devotion, or love of country? Certainly not. When it comes to love, one has to be subjective. If someone loves God and heeds the teachings of the great religions concerning God, it is all for the good. No one is asking us to provide "scientific proof" for the existence or non-existence of God. Certainly in my own religion, Judaism, one is never asked to prove the existence of God. God is, and God does not need to present an ID before entering one's life. There is even a saying in the Talmud, "Would that they forsook Me, but did not forsake My teachings." The rabbis of old understood that what is important in Judaism is not to provide proofs of the existence of a deity, but to do justice, and love mercy, and walk humbly with your creator.

In her recent book *Fields of Blood: Religion and the History of Violence*, Karen Armstrong discusses the current tendency to blame all the outbursts of violence in today's world on religion, pointing to bloody conflicts around the globe which seem to run along the lines of religious conflict. She provides a long historical analysis of religions and civilizations, East and West, and shows how organized human life from the very beginnings of civilization was never able to maintain an orderly and law-abiding society without resorting to violent action.

What Armstrong makes clear is that the main cause of societal violence is not people's religious ideas and practices, but the inequality that has always existed in organized society between the ruling class and the underclasses who were and still are subjugated and exploited. This carries over into acts of terrorism as well, which is why Islamic terrorists today are so at odds with what Islam as a faith should stand for. Same goes for radical Christian groups like the KKK and the Westboro Baptist Church.

The story of humanity is one of unending violent conflicts which are the result of human greed and unwillingness to accommodate the other side. In this grim picture religion at times exerts a moderating influence and at other times plays into the hands of tyrants and corrupt regimes, of which there never seems to be a shortage. One might add that religion is only as good as the people who practice it. If the lofty teachings of the various religions are heeded, much good will result; but if religion is used as a lethal weapon to punish and persecute, it is as evil as those who choose to use their religion in such as way.

But going back to prayer, I have attempted to show in the first part of this book that prayer is a much broader concept than the printed liturgies of the various religions. It is an expression of the human heart that transcends formal religion or formal prayer. And as such, it is also accessible to both atheists and agnostics. Prayer is the yearning of the human heart. It is a cry for help, and it is a cry of joy. It is one of the most normal human expressions of our humanity. A song is a prayer. An act of kindness is a prayer. Righting a wrong is a prayer. It does not matter whether one prays to a higher being or simply opens one's heart to life's possibilities. I pray every waking moment of my life for the welfare of my loved ones and my friends and the people I feel responsible for who, in the greater scheme of things, is the entire human race. And even if my prayer is an illusion, I'd rather be on the side of the greatest illusionist of all times, namely, the immortal Don Quijote de la Mancha, than on the side of skeptics and nay-sayers who think they are better than anyone else.

32. PRAYER FOR FREETHINKERS

There are two religious movements in America which are not God-centered. The first is Unitarianism, which grew out of Christianity in Eastern Europe and came into its own in the United States. The second is Reconstructionism, a progressive Jewish movement born in America as an offshoot of Conservative Judaism. Both movements allow a great deal of latitude to their adherents in religious matters; both have their own liturgies which do not necessarily focus on the deity; and both find meaning in prayer without necessarily praying to God. To the left of these two movements are such organizations as Humanist Judaism, and many humanist societies born out of the Christian religious and secular culture. Those for the most part leave God out of the equation altogether.

As a matter of fact, even within all the theistic movements there are many who are not necessarily believers in God, and yet they seem to be comfortable joining in prayers in which God is invoked repeatedly. It has been my experience over many years of working with children and adults in Jewish schools and synagogues, that some people seem to have what has been recently identified as a "God gene,"* (*) and some do not. This so-called God gene means that the person has an affinity for spirituality, and an awareness of a reality beyond the common physical reality we all share. I believe it is something one is born with, regardless of whether the

*The title of a book by Dean H. Hamer, published 2005.

person is raised in a religious family or a faith community or not. It is similar to having an artistic personality or to having an interest in the wonders of nature or in human history, both recent and ancient. And yet someone who grows up and lives in a community of church-goers or any other type of house of worship attendance would be socially inclined to participate in religious services, regardless of personal belief or disbelief.

It seems to me, however, that someone who is either openly a freethinker, or a closet freethinker, can also find ways to pray, as attested by Unitarians who do not believe in a deity, or, in the case of Jews, Reconstructionist Jews. I recall reading in a Reconstructionist prayer book the blessing for the lighting of the Sabbath candles. The traditional prayer reads:

Blessed are You, O God, king of the universe,
who has sanctified us with Your commandments,
and commanded us to kindle the Sabbath lights.

In the Reconstructionist prayer book this blessing was changed to read:

Blessed is the light in the world.

Here is a Unitarian blessing for breaking bread:

Loving Spirit,
Be our guest,
Dine with us,
Share our bread,

That our table
Might be blessed
And our souls be fed.

Compare this to a traditional Christian prayer before a meal:

Father of us all,
This meal is a sign of Your love for us:
Bless us and bless our food,
And help us to give you glory each day
Through Jesus Christ our Lord.
Amen!

Traditionally, all Christian prayers are filtered through the presence of the Christian Savior. Unitarians, however, do not believe in the trinity, and have their doubts about the traditional concept of the one God. And so God is referred to obliquely as a "loving spirit." In other words, they believe there is something out there which makes a meal not only food for the body, but also food for the spirit. They do feel compelled to say a blessing before they eat, because they do believe in the spiritual dimension of life, and they do use the word "blessed," which is a religious or a spiritual term. The same is true of Jewish Reconstructionists—they too use the word "blessed." To them light is not only a physical presence, but also something spiritual.

I was raised as a secular nationalist Jew in what became the State of Israel when I turned nine. In my school and in my pioneer youth movement, as well as in my home, we did not say the traditional Jewish prayers. My parents left their old-time religion behind when they left Europe. They did sense that something terrible was about to happen to the Jews of Europe, and they saw their parents' religion as a hindrance to becoming a free and secure people. But the new ethos of the new society they and their friends created in the Land of Israel was by no means Marxist or Freudian. It was deeply rooted in Jewish history, Jewish values, and Jewish beliefs. Like the Reconstructionists and the Unitarians, they brought religion or spirituality into our lives through the back door. Here is an example of a poem written by one of our poets of that era, Avraham Shlonsky, which illustrates my point:

> *Dress me my Kosher Mother in a coat of many colors,*
> *And at morning-prayer time take me out to my work.*
> *My land is wrapped in light like a prayer shawl,*
> *Houses are standing like prayer boxes.*
> *The roads our hands have built roll on like tefillin straps.*
> *The fair town thus chants its morning prayer to it maker,*
> *And among the makers is your son Avraham*
> *A road-building poet in the land of Israel.*
> *And at twilight father will return from his labor,*
> *And like a prayer he will whisper contently,*
> *My precious son Avraham,*
> *Skin and sinews and bones,*
> *Hallelujah.*

Shlonsky was born to a Chabad Hasidic family in the Ukraine. Like my parents, he left Europe and he turned his back on his father's religion. If I dare psychoanalyze him by interpreting this poem, I would have to say that he carried inside of him deep guilt feelings for having left the traditional fold. Here he was, a young man in his twenties building roads with his bare hands, as my mother did when she first arrived in Palestine in 1931. The poem shows that he was steeped in Jewish religious observance and in Jewish lore, and he saw himself and the land around him through the filter of that old faith. He was picking up where Joseph and his coat of many colors had left off. He was rebuilding the land of his ancestors not by waiting for the messiah in Europe where the messiah never came, but by building a new future for his people. Here this poet who played a leading role in the revival of the Hebrew language (he coined many new Hebrew words) is telling his mother, who is also mother earth, and his father, who lived a life of prayer, that he too is praying by restoring the land. Here Shlonsky teaches us that prayer is any redemptive act which makes the world better, not only words repeated by rote. Shlonsky the freethinker comes across in this poem as a deeply religious person, for whom prayer is part of his flesh and bones.

Indeed, as I look back across the years I realize that many of my secular teachers and youth leaders and our poets and thinkers were deeply religious people, without the label of religion. The great socialist ideologue of those days, A. D. Gordon, talked about the "religion of work." In my high school in Haifa, the Hareali School, we had a teacher who was a Jewish thinker named Yosef Schechter, who started a movement of "neo-mystics." Many students were attracted to his teachings and tried to live a more traditional Jewish life. In many ways, that generation of Jewish socialists, was much more genuinely spiritual that many a normative religious Jew of today.

Here is an example of a universal prayer for peace which is purely secular:

If there is peace in the heart
There will be peace in the home.
If there is peace in the home,
There will be peace in the community.
If there is peace in the community
There will be peace in the city.
If there is peace in the city
There will be peace in the nation.
If there is peace in the nation
There will be peace in the world.
Let there be peace, and let it begin with me.

What human cause can be more important than peace? Too many people who call themselves believers and spend much time praying see the world as "them and us," "us" of course being the good people, and "them" the evil people we must guard against and if necessary go to war against. Many people, on the other hand, who call themselves secularists and free thinkers are pacifists who accept war only when no other recourse is available. To me a peace-loving person is a spiritual person, one whom God would consider a good person, while a so-called God-fearing person who is belligerent and who believes in war without taking the time to look for other solutions is God-fearing in name only. No prayer to me is more important than a prayer for peace. In the Hebrew language the word *shalom*, or peace, is the most important word next to the word God. The *Kaddish*, the most important word in Jewish liturgy, ends with the words:

May He who makes peace in the heavens above,
Make peace for all of us and for all Israel,
And let us say, Amen.

I would add the words, "and for all humankind."

33. PRAYER AS A WAY OF LIFE

More often than not, prayer is a perfunctory activity. I am not referring only to those who attend prayer services occasionally because of social pressure or some other extraneous reason. I am speaking mainly of those who pray regularly, and believe that by the mere act of sitting in a pew and going through the words of the prayer book they are actually praying. But then there are those to whom prayer is the most important activity in their life. Prayer punctuates their lives and gives it form and order. They cannot conceive of a life without prayer. To them, prayer is the ultimate conversation with the ultimate interlocutor. Without it, their life is empty and devoid of meaning. With it, their life acquires meaning.

Chief among those people are those in all the major religions who devote their life to the service of God, be they monks, nuns, mystics, and so on. They can also be ordinary people, men and women, who feel the presence of God in their lives from the moment they wake up in the morning to the moment they go to sleep at night. They never wander aimlessly through life. They are always anchored in this ultimate reality and they are never alone.

The thought that prayer can fill up a person's life to such a degree makes us realize how great the power of prayer can be. Man, it seems, must have been praying since the beginning of time, and will pray until the end of time. One of the most remarkable books I have ever read was Thomas Merton's classic, *The Seven Storey Mountain*. In his youth, Merton was a student of literature at Columbia University in New York City. But at the same time he became a devout

Catholic, and kept searching for a closer relationship with God. His search took him to a Trappist monastery, where he became a Trappist monk. As you read about his experience of praying and meditating for hours on end you begin to realize that this highly literate, highly sensitive young man found a new life which might be referred to as a "life of prayer." Merton writes:

This business of saying the office on the Erie train, going up through the Delaware valley, was to become a familiar experience in the year that was ahead. . . God began to fill my soul with grace in those days, grace that sprung from deep within me, I could not know how or where. But yet I would be able, after not so many months, to realize what was there, in the peace and the strength that were growing in me through my constant immersion in this tremendous, unending cycle of prayer, ever renewing its vitality, its inexhaustible, sweet energies, from hour to hour, from season to season in it returning round. And I, drawn into that atmosphere, into that deep, vast universal movement of revitalizing prayer, which is Christ praying in men to His Father, could not help but begin at last to live, and to know that I was alive. (pp. 302-3)

Merton had given up a promising literary career in New York for a monastic life in the hills of Kentucky. He became an inspiration for many throughout the world who were searching for meaning in their lives, especially after the end of World War Two, when many young Catholic Americans and others came home from the war with more questions than answers. His life and his testimony are proof that prayer can transform a person, bring greater harmony into one's life and a greater closeness to nature and to the ineffable, and provide the serenity we alluded to in the beginning of this book when we discussed the so-called Serenity Prayer.

Another person who devoted his entire life to prayer and, by doing so, also gave up a promising career, was someone I have known my entire adult life, and who has had a great impact on my own life. I am referring to Rabbi Shlomo Carlebach of blessed memory.

I first met Reb Shlomo, as we used to call him affectionately, at the dormitory of the Hebrew Union College in Cincinnati, Ohio. It was a most unlikely encounter. The school was the citadel of Reform Judaism in America, a Jewish denomination shunned and scorned by Orthodox rabbis like Carlebach. A small notice on our bulletin board announced that a "singing rabbi" was stopping by to sing to us in honor of the upcoming holiday of Purim. We did not know what to expect, but after dinner all of us, students and faculty, filled the "bumming room" lounge of our dorm and waited for our guest.

In walked a roly-poly man in his late thirties holding a guitar, a most unexpected instrument to be played by an Orthodox rabbi in those days. He had a scraggly short black beard and bright black eyes. A hush fell over the audience. Carlebach planted himself in the middle of the room, strapped on his guitar, and began to tune the instrument. He closed his eyes and began to sway back and forth, and if you listened closely you could hear a soft hum. It was the Hasidic way of getting ready to pray.

And pray he did. It turned out he had borrowed lines

from the prayer book or from the Bible and wrote his own melodies which were so contagious we were immediately swept away by their beauty and soulfulness. I noticed that even Dr. Reines, our philosophy professor, who had little use for Jewish Orthodoxy and offered his own new version of Judaism called Polydoxy, and who sat there with a skeptical look on his face, began to tap his fingers on the armrest of the couch. The rest of us were soon singing along and clapping to the rhythm of the song which I still remember after all these years:

You were their salvation forever,
And their hope for all generations.

Only two lines from the traditional Purim text, repeated by Carlebach over and over again, each time with more fervor, each time louder, until all of us, rational Reform rabbinical students, jumped up on our feet and began to dance wildly around the room like Hasidim on Purim after they had two or three glasses of schnapps.

Little did I know that evening I was witnessing a new era in Jewish liturgical music being born, an era ushered in by Reb Shlomo who spent the next thirty years promoting his music and bringing young Jews all over the world back to Judaism. I used to run into him over the years, mainly in synagogues around the country where he came with a small band of young musicians and mesmerized Jewish audiences. I used to run into him on the streets of Manhattan, and he would always hug me and ask me if my prayer life was going well. Most importantly, I saw him perform before half a million Jews in front of the United Nations building in New

York City when we held a rally to free the Jews of the Soviet
Union. He sang his song *Am Yisroel Chai*, The People of
Israel Live, with half a million voices joining in, a song which
next to *hatikvah* has since become the hymn of the Jewish
people everywhere.

I later learned that Carlebach had started out as a disciple
of the great late Lubavicher Rebbe, Rabbi Menachem
Mendel Schneerson of Chabad fame. He was a brilliant
student, and he was slated to become a Rosh Yeshivah, the
head of a Talmudic academy. But Carlebach could not be
confined to old routines. He knew he lived at a time, namely,
the sixties, when many young Jews in America and around
the world were leaving the fold and losing their way. He
loved his people passionately, and he believed in the power
of prayer. He went off on his own while being criticized by
his own people as a pseudo-Orthodox who took drugs and
hugged women, but he kept composing his now- classical
melodies and singing them everywhere. Like Merton, he
lived a life of prayer. Even when he was sitting quietly in a
corner, I could tell he was praying and singing inside. When
he spoke, he would say a few words and suddenly his talk
became a hum and turned into song, a prayer-song or a
musical speech. Now, as I travel around the world, I hear
his neo-Hasidic songs everywhere. When I walk the streets
of Tel Aviv or Jerusalem at night I hear his songs playing on
people's balconies and at weddings and Bar Mitzvahs. The
praying soul of my Reb Shlomo has become the soul of the
Jewish people.

I have offered two contemporary examples of the life of
prayer, one Catholic and one Jewish. We can find similar

examples in all the major religions, be it Buddhist monks or Muslim Sufis and so on. I must admit I envy both Merton and Carlebach. They are my spiritual heroes in a world that has become too materialistic, crass, and profane. We need more people like them. All the major religions need them. Countries that have become overly-secular, like France and the UK and, yes, also Israel, need them. We are living at a time when the life of the spirit is being stifled by technology, and fanatic elements in the name of religion are terrorizing the world. The voices and the works and the prayers of a Mother Theresa, a Martin Luther King, Jr., a Thomas Merton, and a Shlomo Carelbach are drowned by those who commit murder and meyham across the globe. The life of true and sincere prayer must resonate throughout the world if there is any hope for our tortured and violated planet.

Over the years I have lived in four countries around the globe. In all four I witnessed a struggle for human rights and human dignity. I was born in what Christians call the Holy land, and what became in 1948, when I was nine, the State of Israel. From the end of World War Two in 1945, to the end of 1947, I witnessed young Jewish men and women fighting against the British occupation of our land. In fact, we Jews and our Arab neighbors in the city of Haifa lived in harmony. They were not our enemy. The enemy were the foreign occupiers, first the Turks, who for 400 years oppressed the Arabs of Palestine and of the Middle East, and then the British, who defeated the Turks in World War One and were given a mandate over the Holy Land by the League of Nations. For us, colonialism continued until May 15, 1948, when the last British soldier left our land. Poorly armed and with meagre resources, we had to face seven invading Arab armies the next day, when a second Holocaust was about to take place. I for one believe that we prevailed with the help of God, who could not bear to see another Holocaust happen. I believe we had to pray with our puny weapons to survive, as did Joshua and the Israelites when then came to the Promised Land.

In my late teens I lived for four years in Uruguay, a beautiful small country in South America. It was before the days of the Latin American Catholic social protest movement known as Liberation Theology. That movement, which involved many Catholic priests, emerged against the wishes of the Vatican and the Catholic hierarchy because of the abject poverty and the political repression that typified Latin America in those days, and still does.

Uruguay was not nearly as extreme as some of the other countries of Latin America, which were run by ruthless dictators and where most people went to bed hungry. But it was going into economic decline because of the world markets which never seemed to favor Latin America.

I remember how in 1959 a 36-year-old man overthrew one of those dictators and infused all of Latin America with new hope. His name was Fidel Castro, and the dictator he overthrew was Fulgenio Batista of Cuba. I was twenty years old. I was about to go to college in the United States. Someone in Montevideo, Uruguay, called me and told me to come over to the Victoria Plaza Hotel in downtown Montevideo to meet two emissaries of Fidel Castro, who were planning a victory trip through Latin America for the new hero of their country and the great new hope of the continent.

I have never before been inside Uruguay's premier hotel. I went up with my friends through the red carpeted corridors to a luxurious suite and we waited for the Cubans. Two men walked in. They were wearing the olive green uniform of the Cuban revolutionaries, with black berets and red insignia, and they both had black beards, Castro style, which were rare in those days in Latin America.

We heard about their plans to travel with the young hero from Venezuela all the way down to Argentina, and transform the entire continent to socialism, equality, and opportunities for all the *pobres de la tierra*, all the poor of the earth. There was truly something messianic about the whole thing.

But it was not meant to be. Soon we learned that Fidel Castro, under the influence of his brother Raul, became a communist and a client of the Soviet Union. The victory crusade through Latin America never took place. Cuba became isolated by the United States, and in Latin America it was business as usual. So much for youthful idealism.

I went to school in the United States, to the Hebrew Union College in Cincinnati, Ohio, and the University of Cincinnati across the street. I came face to face with a very racist and old fashioned United States. Little did I know at the time the good old U.S.A. was on the verge of a social revolution that would change this country forever. It was the beginning of the sixties, a decade that changed life in the U.S. more than any other decade in the past one hundred years. Three revolutions were afoot at the same time: the peace movement born out of a wide-spread opposition among young Americans against the Vietnam War; the women's liberation movement, seeking equality for woman in the workplace and more control over their own lives; and the struggle for civil rights for African Americans.

In 1965, upon my ordination as rabbi, I was sent by the Union of American Hebrew Congregations (now Union of Reform Judaism) to serve for three years as rabbi in Guatemala. I arrived with my young family in Guatemala in the middle of a civil war. In Latin America civil wars, which are frequent, happen for two reasons: political repression and poverty. Guatemala has experienced both. Moreover, the wealth of the country was in the hands of a few, followed by a small middle class, and at the bottom of the pyramid a vast indigenous population of Mayan Indians and mixed-race Ladinos living at a subsistence level. Clearly, Central America, of which Guatemala was part, was even poorer and more repressed than Uruguay.

When I returned to the United States in 1968, it was no longer the same country I had left in 1965. It was the year both Martin Luther King, Jr. and Robert Kennedy were assassinated. Blacks were rioting in every city in America. The anti-Vietnam War movement was descending on Washington, and later militant feminists like my daughter were too. By 1970, the U.S. was entering a new era of profound social change, and yet the disenfranchisement of minority races and discrimination against women and the LGBT community as well are still major issues, and as for foreign conflicts, the U.S. continues to be enmeshed in those around the world.

This brings us back to our main topic, namely, prayer. My far-ranging life experience leads me to conclude that human history continues to be a struggle in which the entire human race is caught up. Despite the miracles of technology such as the Internet and space travel and laser surgery, there is still vast poverty and violence around the globe. Entire nations with many millions of people such as Myanmar and Syria and North Korea and Cuba are not free and are yet to find their rightful place in the family of nations.

It will take a great deal of human effort to change all of this. But here again we see why prayer continues to be such a powerful expression of human yearning for freedom, for equality, and for a better future for the coming generations. Human beings need to articulate their faith in a better future and their hope that it will come about soon. Prayer is the answer to despair. It is an expression of optimism, of inner fortitude in the face of seemingly insurmountable odds. The Jewish prayer says: we know it takes a long time for salvation to come, but we do not give up hope that indeed it will come.

34. A NEW LANGUAGE OF PRAYER

Nothing has brought more hope, comfort, and solace to the human heart than prayer, and yet nothing in our time needs more revision than prayer. I have alluded to this several times in this book, and as we are nearing the end of the book, I would like to take a closer look at what is needed to make prayer more vital and more responsive to "what the world needs now."

According to the popular American song, "what the world needs now is love, sweet love." This has always been true and always will. Most songs people everywhere sing are about love. Most prayers are also about love, mainly love of God. There is an old saying, "Love conquers all" or, as the Roman poet Virgil has put it, *omnia vincit amor*. And yet therein lies the problem of human existence. Love is so obvious, so natural, and yet so hard to find. So many marriages today end up in divorce. So many families suffer from conflicts among their members. So many people seem not to be able to get along with one another. So much violence plagues people everywhere.

There seems to be a disconnect between life and prayer. Perhaps there always was, but that does not mitigate the urgency of the problem facing the world today. If we were to assess the efficacy of prayer and of religion in general over the ages, I would sum it up as follows: religion and prayer have helped countless people personally and communally in overcoming the many problems of life people face on a daily basis. But religion and prayer have not been able to bring about a world of peace and harmony among the denizens of this earth. People of all faiths have—and still do—bend religion to suit their own purposes to the detriment of others. More often than not, religion has been "the last refuge of the scoundrel." I should know. I have been a member of the clergy now for over fifty years.

Religion always seems to have its built-in vulnerabilities. It is expected to pursue a path of piety and virtue in a world that is dominated by cold and calculating individuals and organizations, both governmental, public and private, who more often than not sacrifice the common good for gain and self-interest. Those clergy who serve congregations are often faced with the need to compromise their principles and convictions to please the lay leaders of their flock. I once had a president of my congregation say to me, "We expect our rabbi to take strong stands on important issues, but we will let you know which issues."

Not all clergy act as a rubber stamp to their lay leaders, doing the bidding of their bosses, and not all lay leaders expect their so-called "spiritual leader" to be a yes-person. Most importantly, many people today, both clergy and laity, are deeply aware of the dire world situation in this early part of the twenty-first century. The world has never before had the kind of access to worldwide communications we have today. Anyone who pays even cursory attention to world news has a good picture of the current condition of the human race. We are constantly bombarded with news from every corner of the world, and what we get certainly does not paint a pretty picture.

What the world needs today is a new language of prayer—an honest, inclusive and effective liturgy that can move people to do the right thing. Granted, prayer all by itself cannot attain such a formidable goal. It needs the other two ingredients we have discussed earlier, namely, the right knowledge and righteous action. In the language of traditional Judaism, the world stands on three things—Torah, prayer, and good deeds. Torah stands for the right knowledge, which is primarily the knowledge of good and evil. If a person cannot tell good from evil, then the prayers of such a person have no meaning. Moreover, such a person is not likely to do good deeds. Doing good and shunning evil is taught by every religion. Those who use their religion and their prayers to do evil are the ones who give prayer and religion a bad name.

We do not need to replace the Torah or the New Testament or the Quran or the scriptures of the Eastern religions. What we need to do is see them in a new light. They have always been open to interpretation, and they have all been interpreted by their respective sages whose interpretations were accepted by their followers—not always readily and willingly, but overtime those interpretations reached a consensus and caught up with the changing times.

What often happens with religion, though, is that it tends to become frozen in time and lose touch with new realities. To the detriment of many Muslim societies, they have been lagging behind the Western world and resisted change. Protestantism has had its reformers in past centuries and still does, while Catholicism, which has held out long into the twentieth century, has been reforming itself for the past fifty years. As for Judaism, it has also undergone a transformation in Europe and in North America since the nineteenth century, with the emergence of such new movements as Reform, Conservative, and Reconstructionist Judaism. There has been some modernization in some

Orthodox Jewish movements, but for the most part Jewish Orthodoxy and particularly ultra-Orthodoxy have much catching up to do. The same is true of some Christian fundamentalist denominations and sects which have become more conservative.

Given the current state of the human race, it seems to me that the vast majority of the followers of the major world religions would welcome new approaches to the beliefs and practices of their respective faiths which will help change the way each faith perceives and interacts with all the others. Such new approaches will be reflected in the text of the prayers or the liturgy of the respective faiths.

In other words, we need a new language of prayer which is not sectarian, tribal, or territorial, which is not about "them" and "us," but which embraces all people and all life on this planet. Nowhere have I found a nobler expression of this truth than in the Jain religion, which offers the following prayer:

May you, O Revered One! Voluntarily permit me. I would like to confess my sinful acts committed while walking. I honor your permission. I desire to absolve myself of the sinful acts by confessing them. I seek forgiveness from all those living beings which I may have tortured while walking, coming and going, treading on living organism, seeds, green grass, dew drops, ant hills, moss, live water, live earth, spider web and others. I seek forgiveness from all these living beings, be they—one sensed, two sensed, three sensed, four sensed or five sensed. Which I may have kicked, covered with dust, rubbed with ground, collided with

other, turned upside down, tormented, frightened,
shifted from one place to another or killed and deprived
them of their lives. (By confessing) may I be absolved
of all these sins.

The sentiment expressed in this prayer is common to Eastern religions, particularly to Buddhism. Here we have a perfect example of a prayer which, if incorporated in all the liturgies of the world, will take the world a giant step forward towards a new language of universal prayer that can do no harm to anyone but rather help all people achieve enlightenment.

During the Holocaust, the Nazi regime of Germany introduced a race theory which divided the human race into "super-humans" and "sub-humans." Germans and other West and North Europeans were superior, while Slavs, Blacks, gypsies, homosexuals, and particularly Jews were inferior. The inferior people were expendable and were considered detrimental to society so they could be rooted out with impunity. This godless race theory flew in the face of all the teaching of all the major religions of the world. Neither Moses nor Jesus nor Muhammad and certainly not the Buddha believed in inferior and superior people. They all maintained that all living beings deserve respect and compassion. They all believed that life is sacred. The foregoing Jain prayer posits the sanctity of all life, and makes it clear that those who willfully destroy life are enemies of the "Revered One."

In the new universal language of prayer the sanctity of life should be the first and foremost guiding principle. All else should flow from this principle. In other words, the emphasis should be shifted from "I am the Lord your God," which is the first of the Ten Commandments, or "there is no God but Allah," which is the declaration of faith of Islam, or Christianity's "in the name of the father and the son and the holy spirit," to "Life is sacred, because it is the work of God." In other words, instead of focusing on extolling God, prayer should focus on extolling life, which is the work of God. This is in keeping with traditional Jewish thinking, where we find the statement attributed to God, "I would rather they forsook Me but kept my teaching." It is certainly in keeping with the teaching of the New Testament, where we find the statement, "whatever you did for one of the least of my brothers and sisters, you did for me," (Matt. 25:40) and also with the teaching of the Qur'an where it says, ". . .take not life which Allah has made sacred" (al-An'am 6:151).

More than craving praise, God craves our respect for God's handiwork from the lowest form of life to the highest. This critical point, which is central to Eastern religions like Jainism, is not emphasized enough in the Western religions. The liturgies of the Western monotheistic religions focus on glorifying, exalting, praising, thanking, and reminding God over and over again that God is great and we humans are hardly worthy of God's attention and mercy. Where those religions come up short is in not paying enough attention to what Judaism believes to be the unique place of the human race in God's creation, namely, a partner in the work of creation. To follow the biblical stories of creation, God did not create man as a helpless creature, quite the opposite. God says to Adam and Eve, "Fill the earth and master it." (Gen 1:28) Or, in the words of the psalmist, God made man "a little less than divine" (8:5-6):

What is man, that You remember of him?
or the son of man, that You visit him?
You have made him a little lower than divine,
You have crowned him with honor and glory.

In other words, man is not so helpless, and man does not need to praise God constantly. The rabbis say: "Speak little and do much." (Pirke Avot 1:14) Those who spend a great deal of time praying and exalting God do not necessarily do much good. Once again, "God helps those who help themselves." I would take this timeless saying a step further and add, ". . . and who also help others."

In short, in the new language of prayer there will be less emphasis on praising God and more emphasis on doing God's will, namely, helping others and being mindful of the sanctity of all life on this planet. This would be a huge step forward in making life livable on this planet.

One mistake Western religions have been making since their inception is institutionalizing poverty. All three speak of charity, which basically translates into "alms for the poor." Christianity goes a step further and glorifies poverty, since "it is easier for a poor person to enter the kingdom of heaven than for a rich person." None of the three has put forth the idea that poverty can be eradicated, if only society put its mind to it. The "War on Poverty" which was declared in the United States in the late sixties and is yet to be won should be another key concept of the new language of prayer. The praying person must be reminded again and again that poverty is not here to stay but must be eradicated.

When I was a child growing up in what became Israel, we pre-state Jews would not allow anyone to go hungry. This was a custom we brought with us from the old country. I remember my mother telling me that if I did not finish my sandwich I should put it out on the fence so that if a hungry person passed by she or he may take it.

In the twentieth century new ideologies, mainly communism, sought to establish a world without hunger or want, but failed. In all the three democracies I have lived in, namely, Israel, Uruguay, and the U.S., there are many people today who go to bed hungry. It reminds me of the American prayer song, "It's me O Lord standing in the need of prayer." Yes, as long as we allow people in our communities and in our country to go to bed hungry we all stand in need of prayer. We certainly should incorporate this prayer in our new language of prayer.

Another critical area of human interaction which has come to the fore in our time is the rights of women. There are still many places in the world today where women are not treated as equals. Not enough attention has been given to this problem in the prayer book. This too needs to be reflected in the new liturgical language. As was discussed earlier, the monotheistic God has been always presented as an all-powerful male figure, referred to as a father or a king. And yet, Judaism makes it quite clear that God is neither male nor female, indeed, has no gender. This critical point seems to have been lost on most people, and has contributed to the treatment of women as second class members of society.

To me, the common use of the word Lord in English to describe God is antiquated and unfair to women. In England, where the title Lord originated, it no longer has much meaning, while in other parts of the English-speaking world there is no such title. A new way of referring to God is needed which will take into account the rights of women and will be all-inclusive.

Another area of human life which religion seems to have institutionalized is warfare. As was discussed in the chapter about prayer and war, man since the beginning of time has prayed to God or the gods for victory in war and has envisioned the deity as warlike. In the Hebrew Bible we find the reference to God as a "man of war." God was believed to take sides in war and to this day we find Jewish, Christian and Muslim clergy invoking God's help in time of war.

This is another area of prayer where a change is needed. Even though sometimes war in necessary for defensive purposes it should not be looked upon as something God may take part in or condone. Like slavery and like discrimination against women, war as an object of prayer should no longer be countenanced. Instead, a sincere yearning for peace should be emphasized when pushed into waging war, and every effort should be made to minimize the damage of war.

Another concept that has been greatly emphasized in all the liturgies of the West is that of sin. These liturgies have generally looked upon man as sinful by nature, as stated in the opening stories of the Book of Genesis: "The inclination of man's heart from his youth is evil" (8:21) Christianity has taken this a step further by positing that man is born in sin, and needs to be saved. Over time, sin has been used as a weapon to intimidate the believers and threaten them with damnation if they did not fall into line. Here too, some thought needs to be given to whether this attitude has done more harm than good.

The traditional concept of sin has made fear the basis of faith. What needs to be revisited here is the belief that man is born in sin. The broader outlook is that man is born with the capacity for both good and evil. The vast majority of the human race is not patently sinful and evil. It is true that a few evil people can inflict great harm on others, and need to be dealt with. But the presumption that people in general are sinful or evil is counterproductive. Instead of dwelling on sin in our liturgies the emphasis should be shifted to human proclivity to err, and to the idea that to "forgive is divine." God does not desire the death of the wrongdoer, but rather that the wrongdoer mend his or her ways and be forgiven (Ezekiel 23:10).

In short, prayer needs to be made more humane and more people-friendly. There comes a moment when, confronting what might be referred to as bottomless evil, there is no choice but to resort to some harsh language in condemning evil. But those are extreme moments. The main thrust of prayer needs to be redemptive and constructive.

Another critical area of our lives, more critical today than ever before in history, is the physical condition of our planet. Our planet, the earth which God gave us, is in a worse condition today than it has been since perhaps the ice age. Much of this is due to human action. I have traveled the globe in the past twelve years, and I have seen the rain forest of the Amazon depleted and its wildlife diminished. I have seen the coral reefs of the world, from the islands of the Caribbean Sea to the Red Sea to the Far East pulverized and turned into white underwater cemeteries. I have seen elephants and other wildlife in Africa mutilated and decimated by poachers. And I have seen urban blight everywhere.

The psalmist said centuries ago: "The earth is the Lord's and the fullness thereof." (24:1) *We* are not the masters of nature. God is. We are the custodians who must care for nature and pass it down to future generations. This precious trust must be emphasized in the new language of prayer. Here again we learn from the Jain religion and from other Eastern religions how to treasure and protect every living thing. Here too we need new liturgical language that will keep reminding us of this sacred trust.

These are but some of the areas of human life which need to become central in human prayer. It should be clear to any caring person in today's world that in our lifetime profound changes have been taking place in the human condition, any they need to be incorporated in the new language of prayer, if prayer is to become the source of inspiration and inner fortitude it was meant to be.

35. A BLUEPRINT FOR THE FUTURE

A person's life consists of many narratives. Sometimes I feel I have lived not one lifetime but several. We all go through life following a daily routine, and it seems as though we live one uniform life. But this is only an illusion designed to keep us focused on the task at hand. In reality, our life consists of many strands that weave in and out of our daily reality as we go through the days and through the years. Now that I have lived more than three-quarters of a century, have travelled to most of the countries of the world, have had several careers, and have written some 60 books on various subjects, I have a life history more complex than most people's. I look back at my multicultural and multifaceted life and, as a native of that tiny land that gave the world the religions followed by more than half of the human race, most notably the three so-called Abrahamic religions, I begin to recall other, less known religions, with which I have had close encounters since a very young age.

Of particular interest for our present discussion on prayer is a religion whose world center happened to be next door to the house I grew up in in my hometown of Haifa. This little-known religion is called the Baha'i Faith. It is small in numbers, but it has a broader vision than any other religion I have ever known.

In this concluding chapter I would like to go back to my childhood and engage in "what if." What if that little-known religion I remember from my early life had managed to persuade the other religions of the world that some of its key concepts are correct? What if it were able to teach the world to sing in perfect harmony the following familiar song,

Come on, people now
Smile on your brother
Everybody get together
Try to love one another right now

Back to my hometown and my early years.

Haifa is one of those cities endowed with a natural beauty that takes one's breath away. It begins at the seashore of the east Mediterranean Sea alongside a large semi-circular bay that ends in the north with the promontory of the historical town of Acre. It then climbs up and around Mount Carmel, the mountain where the prophet Elijah challenged his people during the reign of King Ahab to return to the God of Israel. Everywhere you go in Haifa you see scenic views of the sea and the mountain slopes and the rising streets.

But the most celebrated sight of Haifa are the Baha'i Gardens with their steps climbing all the way from the Lower City to a high point up the mountain, leading to a magnificent white marble temple with a golden dome known as the Baha'i World Center. That temple was a few minutes' walk from my old home on Arlozorov Street, where, as a young child, I used to take walks through the temple's Persian gardens, where I was particularly attracted to their beautifully cultivated cacti beds which had turned me into a lifelong lover of those exotic plants. As I recall, there was little activity in that temple, which most of the time was unattended, except for a guard, and which was surrounded by an air of mystery.

One day I saw an English-speaking man with white hair and a ruddy face standing at the temple's gate. He was passing out pamphlets explaining the nature of the Baha'i

Faith. I read the pamphlet and found out that the followers of the Baha'u'llah, the founder and prophet of the Baha'i Faith, who was buried in Acre, or Akko, across the bay from Haifa, believed that all the founders of the major religions, such as Moses and Jesus and Muhammad and the Buddha and all the rest, were true messengers of the word of the one God, and all of them were respected by the Baha'i believers as true prophets. I remember that even as a young teenager with very little knowledge of religions, including my own, I was fascinated by this concept. I knew back then that each religion considered itself to be the true one, and I thought the Baha'is were on to something that was quite intriguing.

Years later, when I became a student of religions, I rediscovered the Baha'i Faith. Once again, I found out it was different from Islam, from whose bosom it had sprung, and from both Christianity and Judaism. Those three are what I would call militant religions, not to say triumphalist, as we have discussed earlier. To this day, Islam and Christianity are locked in a worldwide struggle, while both have been less than kind to Judaism. The Baha'i Faith, on the other hand, is the exact opposite. Its entire ideology is geared towards finding a common language of faith, reconciliation, and unity among the religions of the world. Lofty goals indeed, which make one wonder if such a thing is possible.

Given today's world situation, few people would think such things possible. And yet, the Baha'is may have the answer to the future of the human race. Since the early part of the twentieth century, humanity has been on the path of self-destruction. Despite two world wars and countless local wars in the past one hundred years, weapons are being constantly upgraded at an enormous cost, new conflicts keep flaring up around the world, and innocent people are being massacred every day.

And yet, humanity continues to yearn and pray for a world at peace. What many people would be surprised to find out is that the faith that has been actively pursuing world peace for the past two centuries was started in Persia, today's Iran, by a Shi'a Muslim named Mirza Husayn-Ali Nuri, born in Tehran in 1817. Under the name Bahá'u'lláh (Glory of God), the founder of the Baha'i Faith claimed to be a prophet who fulfilled the teachings of the Bab, meaning the symbolic "Gate" between past ages of prophecy and a new age of fulfilment for humanity. He further promoted himself as the fulfilment of the messianic expectations of the major religions, notably Islam and Christianity.

Having studied the Baha'i Faith now for some time, I have come to the conclusion that this belief system is not just another form of religion like all the rest, but something altogether different. It posits that God, the Creator of the Universe, cultivates intellectual and moral capacities through the progressively revealed teachings of His messengers. In fact, the Baha'i leadership is quite active in UN agencies that provide help and relief around the world. The guiding principles of the Baha'i Faith sound like a credo for its goals. They are:

Unity of God across all the religions
Unity of all religions
Unity of the entire human race
Unity across the diversity of the human race
Equality between men and women
Elimination of all forms of prejudice

World peace and a new world order
Harmony of religion and science
An ever-advancing Civilization
Universal Independent investigation of truth
Universal compulsory education
A Universal auxiliary language
Obedience to government unless submission to its laws
amounts to a denial of Faith
Elimination of extremes of wealth and poverty

These are very lofty goals, and one could easily argue that they are not attainable. John Lennon envisioned these principles in his famous poem Imagine, which he takes a step further by suggesting that religion should be abolished altogether, with which I disagree. I do, however, agree with the late great singer and song writer when he asks us to image all people living in peace as a brotherhood of man with nothing to kill or die for.

The spirit the Baha'i writings is reflected in the following Baha'i prayer:

Be generous in prosperity
and thankful in adversity.
Be fair in thy judgment
and guarded in thy speech.
Be a lamp unto those who walk in darkness
and a home to the stranger.
Be eyes to the blind
and a guiding light unto the feet of the erring.
Be a breath of life to the body of humankind,
a dew to the soil of the human heart,
and a fruit upon the tree of humility.

It seems to me that if the human race could reach this level of perfection, envisioned two centuries ago by the Baha'u'llah, this would indeed become a world worth living in. In the meantime we can only dream. It is remarkable that all the people of good will in this world have this dream, but it is the fanatics and the troublemakers who for now seem to win the day. The best example is the case of the Baha'is themselves. In Iran, the country where this faith originated, they are being persecuted. In the rest of the world they are hardly noticed, and most people have never heard of them.

Yet one is allowed to dream. What would life be without dreams? What will we be passing on to our children? Do we want them to live in the kind of world we are living in? Would we want them not to dream of a better world?

Perhaps the Baha'i by themselves cannot make the world see the need for their vision to be fulfilled. But I have a proposition for the religions of the world. I would like to propose that the Baha'i guiding principles be seriously considered by all the major faiths, and that a dialogue be initiated among all of us to look for ways to bring the world together.